The Bourgeois Gentleman

DOVER·THRIFT·EDITIONS

The Bourgeois Gentleman

MOLIÈRE

DOVER PUBLICATIONS, INC.
Mineola, New York

DOVER THRIFT EDITIONS

GENERAL EDITOR: PAUL NEGRI
EDITOR OF THIS VOLUME: JOHN BERSETH

Theatrical Rights

This Dover Thrift Edition may be used in its entirety, in adaptation, or in any other way for theatrical productions, professional and amateur, in the United States, without fee, permission, or acknowledgment. (This may not apply outside of the United States, as copyright conditions may vary.)

Bibliographical Note

This Dover edition, first published in 2001, contains the unabridged text of *Le Bourgeois Gentilhomme*, based on the 18th-century translation from the French by H. Baker and J. Miller. A new Note has been added.

Library of Congress Cataloging-in-Publication Data

Molière, 1622–1673.
    [Bourgeois gentilhomme. English.]
    The bourgeois gentleman / Molière.
       p. cm.
    ISBN 0-486-41592-9 (pbk.)
    I. Title.

PQ1829 .A418 2001
842'.4—dc21

00-052304

Manufactured in the United States of America
Dover Publications, Inc., 31 East 2nd Street, Mineola, N.Y. 11501

Note

"MOLIÈRE" was the pseudonym of the French actor-manager and dramatist Jean Baptiste Poquelin (1622-1673). Born in Paris and educated at the Jesuit College de Clermont, Molière abandoned his studies and the prospect of a court appointment to form the company of the Illustre Theatre in 1643. The troupe was not a great success during its two years in the capital—a time when Molière was imprisoned for non-payment of debts—and began touring the French provinces in 1645. During the next dozen or so years Molière developed his theatrical skills to a high degree. His by-now polished company returned to Paris in 1658, under the patronage of Philippe, duc d'Orleans (the brother of King Louis XIV), and performed regularly before enthusiastic audiences. After a series of successful runs at the Petit-Bourbon, the company moved to the Palais-Royal in 1661. The company became the Troupe du roi in 1665.

Le Bourgeois Gentilhomme was first performed for the King's Court at Chambord in 1670, with the playwright in the title role of Monsieur Jourdain. Louis XIV had commissioned the work specifically to lampoon the pomp and pretension, rivaling his own, of the Ottoman Turk envoy to Paris. In addition, the work was to be a ballet comedy written in collaboration with the Court composer, Jean-Baptiste Lully. The resulting production, combining a spoken play with songs and dances, was well received and soon began a public run in Paris. Molière's performance, as usual, won applause from both noble and common audiences. But he was already ill, perhaps worn down by his battle with both church and state over their censorship of *Tartuffe*. Still, Molière was able to write and produce four more plays before his death on stage, on February 17, 1673. In the more than 300 years since then, critics have often praised *Le Bourgeois Gentilhomme* as being strikingly relevant to middle-class life in their own times. Unlike Tartuffe and some other roles created by Molière, M. Jourdain is a sympathetic fellow, more foolish than malevolent, a comic character, especially in contrast to his shrewd and sensible wife.

Contents

Dramatis Personnae

MONSIEUR JOURDAIN — *the bourgeois*
MADAME JOURDAIN — *wife to M. Jourdain*
LUCILE — *daughter to M. Jourdain*
CLÉONTE — *in love with Lucile*
DORIMÈNE — *a marchioness*
DORANTE — *a count, Dorimène's lover*
NICOLE — *a maid-servant to M. Jourdain*
COVIELLE — *servant to Cléonte*
MUSIC MASTER
MUSIC MASTER'S PUPIL
DANCING MASTER
FENCING MASTER
PHILOSOPHY MASTER
MASTER TAILOR
JOURNEYMAN TAILOR
LACKEYS

The scene is in Paris, in M. Jourdain's house

Act I.

Scene I.

MUSIC MASTER, *a* PUPIL *of the* MUSIC MASTER
(*Composing at a table in the middle of the stage*), *a* WOMAN SINGER,
two MEN SINGERS, *a* DANCING MASTER, *and* DANCERS.

MUSIC MASTER. [*To the musicians*] Here, step into this hall, and sit there till he comes.

DANCING MASTER. [*To the dancers*] And you too, on this side.

MUSIC MASTER. [*To his pupil*] Is it done?

PUPIL. Yes.

MUSIC MASTER. Let's see. . . . 'Tis mighty well.

DANCING MASTER. Is it anything new?

MUSIC MASTER. Yes, 'tis an air for a serenade, which I set him to compose here while we wait till our gentleman's awake.

DANCING MASTER. May one see what it is?

MUSIC MASTER. You will hear it, with the dialogue, when he comes. He won't be long.

DANCING MASTER. We have no want of business, either of us, at present.

MUSIC MASTER. 'Tis true. We have found a man here, just such a one as we both of us want. This same Monsieur Jourdain is a sweet income, with his visions of nobility and gallantry which he has got into his noddle, and it would be well for your capers and my crotchets, were all the world like him.

DANCING MASTER. Not altogether so well; I wish, for his sake, that he were better skilled than he is in the things we give him.

MUSIC MASTER. It is true he understands 'em ill, but he pays for 'em well. And that's what our art has more need of at present than of anything else.

DANCING MASTER. For my part, I own it to you, I regale a little

1

upon glory. I am sensible of applause, and think it a very grievous punishment in the liberal arts to display one's self to fools and to expose our compositions to the barbarous judgment of the stupid. Talk no more of it, there is a pleasure in working for persons who are capable of relishing the delicacies of an art, who know how to give a kind reception to the beauties of a work, and, by titillating approbation, regale you for your labour. Yes, the most agreeable recompense one can receive for the things one does is to see them understood, to see 'em caressed with an applause that does you honour. There's nothing, in my opinion, which pays us better than this for all our fatigues. And the praises of connoisseurs give an exquisite delight.

MUSIC MASTER.   I grant it, and I relish them as well as you. There is nothing certainly that tickles more than the applause you speak of, but one cannot live upon this incense. Sheer praises won't make a man easy. There must be something solid mixed withal, and the best method of praising is to praise with the open hand. This indeed is one whose understanding is very shallow, who speaks of everything awry, and cross of the grain, and never applauds but in contradiction to sense. But his money sets his judgment right. He has discernment in his purse. His praises are current coin; and this ignorant commoner is more worth to us, as you see, than that grand witty lord who introduced us here.

DANCING MASTER.   There's something of truth in what you say; but I find you lean a little too much towards the pelf. And mere interest is something so base that an honest man should never discover an attachment to it.

MUSIC MASTER.   For all that, you decently receive the money our spark gives you.

DANCING MASTER.   Certainly; but I don't place all my happiness in that: and I wish that, with his fortune, he had also some good taste of things.

MUSIC MASTER.   I wish the same; 'tis what we both labour at as much as we can. But, however, he gives us the opportunity of making ourselves known in the world; and he'll pay for others what others praise for him.

DANCING MASTER.   Here he comes.

Scene II.

M. JOURDAIN *(in a nightgown and cap)*, PUPIL, DANCING MASTER, MUSIC MASTER, SINGERS, DANCERS, LACKEYS.

M. JOURDAIN.   Well, gentlemen? What have you there? Will you let me see your little drollery?

DANCING MASTER.   How? What little drollery?

M. JOURDAIN.   Why the—how do you call that thing? your pro-
logue, or dialogue of songs and dancing.

DANCING MASTER.   Ha, ha!

MUSIC MASTER.   You see we are ready.

M. JOURDAIN.   I have made you wait a little, but 'tis because I am to
be dressed out to-day like your people of quality; and my hosier has sent
me a pair of silk stockings which I thought I should never have got on.

MUSIC MASTER.   We are here only to wait your leisure.

M. JOURDAIN.   I desire you'll both stay till they have brought me my
clothes, that you may see me.

DANCING MASTER.   As you please.

M. JOURDAIN.   You shall see me most exactly equipped from head
to foot.

MUSIC MASTER.   We don't doubt it.

M. JOURDAIN.   I have had this Indian thing made up for me.

DANCING MASTER.   'Tis very handsome.

M. JOURDAIN.   My tailor tells me that people of quality go thus in a
morning.

MUSIC MASTER.   It fits you to a miracle.

M. JOURDAIN.   Why, ho! Fellow there! both my fellows!

FIRST LACKEY.   Your pleasure, sir?

M. JOURDAIN.   [*To the* MUSIC *and* DANCING MASTERS] What say
you of my liveries?

DANCING MASTER.   They are magnificent.

M. JOURDAIN.   [*Half-opens his gown and reveals a tight pair of
breeches of scarlet velvet, and a green velvet jacket*] Here again is a kind
of dishabille to perform my exercises in a morning.

MUSIC MASTER.   'Tis gallant.

M. JOURDAIN.   Lackey!

FIRST LACKEY.   Sir?

M. JOURDAIN.   T'other lackey!

SECOND LACKEY.   Sir?

M. JOURDAIN.   [*Taking off his gown*] Hold my gown. [*To the* MUSIC
and DANCING MASTERS] Do you like me so?

DANCING MASTER.   Mighty well; nothing can be better.

M. JOURDAIN.   Now for your affair a little.

MUSIC MASTER.   I should be glad first to let you hear an air
[*Pointing to his pupil*] he has just composed for the serenade which you
gave me orders about. He is one of my pupils, who has an admirable
talent for these sort of things.

M. JOURDAIN.   Yes, but that should not have been put to a pupil to
do; you were not too good for that business yourself.

MUSIC MASTER.   You must not let the name of pupil impose upon you, sir. These sort of pupils know as much as the greatest masters, and the air is as good as can be made. Hear it only.

M. JOURDAIN.   [*To his servants*] Give me my gown that I may hear the better.—Stay, I believe I shall be better without the gown.—No, give it me again, it will do better.

MUSICIAN.

> *I languish night and day, nor sleeps my pain,*
> *Since those fair eyes imposed the rigorous chain;*
> *But tell me, Iris, what dire fate attends*
> *Your enemies, if thus you treat your friends?*

M. JOURDAIN.   This song seems to me a little upon the dismal; it inclines one to sleep; I should be glad you could enliven it a little here and there.

MUSIC MASTER.   'Tis necessary, sir, that the air should be suited to the words.

M. JOURDAIN.   I was taught one perfectly pretty some time ago. Stay—um—how is it?

DANCING MASTER.   In good troth, I don't know.

M. JOURDAIN.   There's lamb in it.

DANCING MASTER.   Lamb?

M. JOURDAIN.   Yes—Ho!

> *I thought my dear Namby*
> *As gentle as fair-o:*
> *I thought my dear Namby*
> *As mild as a lamb-y.*
> *Oh dear, oh dear, oh dear-o!*
> *For now the sad scold is a thousand times told,*
> *More fierce than a tiger or bear-o.*

Isn't it pretty?

MUSIC MASTER.   The prettiest in the world.

DANCING MASTER.   And you sing it well.

M. JOURDAIN.   Yet I never learnt music.

MUSIC MASTER.   You ought to learn it, sir, as you do dancing. They are two arts which have a strict connection one with the other.

DANCING MASTER.   And which open the human mind to see the beauty of things.

M. JOURDAIN.   What, do people of quality learn music too?

MUSIC MASTER.   Yes, sir.

M. JOURDAIN.   I'll learn it then. But I don't know how I shall find

time. For, besides the fencing master who teaches me, I have also got
me a philosophy master, who is to begin this morning.

MUSIC MASTER.   Philosophy is something; but music, sir, music—

DANCING MASTER.   Music and dancing—music and dancing, that
is all that's necessary.

MUSIC MASTER.   There's nothing so profitable in a state as music.

DANCING MASTER.   There's nothing so necessary for men as dancing.

MUSIC MASTER.   A state cannot subsist without music.

DANCING MASTER.   Without dancing, a man can do nothing.

MUSIC MASTER.   All the disorders, all the wars one sees in the
world, happen only from not learning music.

DANCING MASTER.   All the disasters of mankind, all the fatal mis-
fortunes that histories are replete with, the blunders of politicians, the
miscarriages of great commanders, all this comes from want of skill in
dancing.

M. JOURDAIN.   How so?

MUSIC MASTER.   Does not war proceed from want of concord
amongst men?

M. JOURDAIN.   That's true.

MUSIC MASTER.   And if all men learnt music, would not that be a
means of keeping them better in tune, and of seeing universal peace in
the world?

M. JOURDAIN.   You're in the right.

DANCING MASTER.   When a man has been guilty of a defect in his
conduct—be it in the affairs of his family, or in the government of the
state, or in the command of an army—don't we always say, such a one
has made a false step in such an affair?

M. JOURDAIN.   Yes, we say so.

DANCING MASTER.   And can making a false step proceed from anything but not knowing how to dance?

M. JOURDAIN.   'Tis true, and you are both in the right.

DANCING MASTER.   This is to let you see the excellence and advantage of dancing and music.

M. JOURDAIN.   I now comprehend it.

MUSIC MASTER.   Will you see each of our compositions?

M. JOURDAIN.   Yes.

MUSIC MASTER.   I have told you already that this is a slight essay
which I formerly made upon the different passions that may be ex-
pressed by music.

M. JOURDAIN.   Very well.

MUSIC MASTER.   [To the MUSICIANS] Here, come forward. [To M.

JOURDAIN] You are to imagine with yourself that they are dressed like
shepherds.

M. JOURDAIN.   Why always shepherds? One sees nothing but such
stuff everywhere.

MUSIC MASTER.   When we are to introduce persons as speaking in
music, 'tis necessary to probability that we give in to the pastoral way.
Singing has always been appropriated to shepherds; and it is by no
means natural in dialogue that princes or citizens should sing their passions.

M. JOURDAIN.   Be it so, be it so. Let's see.

[*Dialogue in music between a Woman and two Men*]

WOMAN.
    The heart that must tyrannic love obey,
    A thousand fears and cares oppress.
    Sweet are those sighs and languishments, they say;
    Say what they will for me,
    Nought is so sweet as liberty.

FIRST MAN.
    Nothing so sweet as love's soft fire,
    Which can two glowing hearts inspire
    With the same life, the same desire.
    The loveless swain no happiness can prove.
    From life take soothing love,
    All pleasure you remove.

SECOND MAN.
    Sweet were the wanton archer's sway,
    Would all with constancy obey;
    But, cruel fate!
    No nymph is true:
    The faithless sex more worthy of our hate,
    To love should bid eternally adieu.

FIRST MAN.
    Pleasing heat!

WOMAN.
    Freedom blest!

SECOND MAN.
    Fair deceit!

FIRST MAN.
    O how I love thee!

WOMAN.
    How I approve thee!

SECOND MAN.
  I detest!
FIRST MAN.
  Against love's ardour quit this mortal hate.
WOMAN.
  Shepherd, myself I bind here,
  To show a faithful mate.
SECOND MAN.
  Alas! but where to find her?
WOMAN.
  Our glory to retrieve,
  My heart I here bestow.
SECOND MAN.
  But, nymph, can I believe
  That heart no change will know?
WOMAN.
  Let experience decide,
  Who loves best of the two.
SECOND MAN.
  And the perjured side
  May vengeance pursue.
ALL THREE.
  Then let us kindle soft desire,
  Let us fan the amorous fire.
  Ah! how sweet it is to love,
  When hearts united constant prove!

M. JOURDAIN.   Is this all?
MUSIC MASTER.   Yes.
M. JOURDAIN.   I find 'tis very concise, and there are some little sayings in it pretty enough.

DANCING MASTER.   You have here, for my composition, a little essay of the finest movements, and the most beautiful attitudes with which a dance can possibly be varied.

M. JOURDAIN.   Are they shepherds too?

DANCING MASTER.   They're what you please. [*To the* DANCERS] Hola!

Act II.

Scene I.

MONSIEUR JOURDAIN, MUSIC MASTER, DANCING MASTER, FOOT-BOY.

M. JOURDAIN.   This is none of your stupid things, and these same fellows flutter it away bravely.

MUSIC MASTER.   When the dance is mixed with the music, it will have a greater effect still, and you will see something gallant in the little entertainment we have prepared for you.

M. JOURDAIN.   That's however for by and by; and the person for whom I have ordered all this, is to do me the honour of dining with me here.

DANCING MASTER.   Everything's ready.

MUSIC MASTER.   But in short, sir, this is not enough, 'tis necessary such a person as you, who live great and have an inclination to things that are handsome, should have a concert of music at your house every Wednesday, or every Thursday.

M. JOURDAIN.   Why so? Have people of quality?

MUSIC MASTER.   Yes, sir.

M. JOURDAIN.   I'll have one then. Will it be fine?

MUSIC MASTER.   Certainly. You must have three voices, a treble, a counter-tenor, and bass, which must be accompanied with a bass-viol, a theorbo-lute, and a harpsichord for the thorough-bass, with two violins to play the symphonies.

M. JOURDAIN.   You must add also a trumpet-marine. The trumpet-marine is an instrument that pleases me, and is very harmonious.

MUSIC MASTER.   Leave us to manage matters.

M. JOURDAIN.   However, don't forget by and by to send the musicians to sing at table.

MUSIC MASTER.   You shall have everything you should have.

M. JOURDAIN.   But above all, let the entertainment be fine.

MUSIC MASTER.   You will be pleased with it, and, amongst other things, with certain minuets you will find in it.

M. JOURDAIN.   Ay, the minuets are my dance; and I have a mind you should see me dance 'em. Come, master.

DANCING MASTER. Your hat, sir, if you please. [M. JOURDAIN *takes off his foot-boy's hat, and puts it on over his own nightcap; upon which his master takes him by the hand and makes him dance to a minuet-air which he sings*]

> Tol, lol, lol, lol, lol, lol,
> Tol, lol, lol,
> > *twice;*
> Tol, lol, lol; tol, lol.
> > > *In time, if you please,*
> Tol, lol,
> > *the right leg.*
> Tol, lol, lol.
> > > *Don't shake your shoulders so much.*
> Tol, lol, lol, lol, lol.
> > > > *Why, your arms are out of joint.*
> Tol, lol, lol, lol, lol.
> > > > > *Hold up your head. Turn out your toes.*
> Tol, lol, lol.
> > > *Your body erect.*

M. JOURDAIN. Heh?

MUSIC MASTER. Admirably well performed.

M. JOURDAIN. Now I think of it, teach me how I must bow to salute a marchioness; I shall have occasion for it by and by.

DANCING MASTER. How you must bow to salute a marchioness?

M. JOURDAIN. Yes, a marchioness whose name is Dorimène.

DANCING MASTER. Give me your hand.

M. JOURDAIN. No. You need only to do it, I shall remember it easily.

DANCING MASTER. If you would salute her with a great deal of respect, you must first of all make a bow and fall back, then advancing towards her, bow thrice, and at the last bow down to her very knees.

M. JOURDAIN. Do it a little. [*After the* DANCING MASTER *has made three bows*] Right.

Scene II.

M. JOURDAIN, MUSIC MASTER, DANCING MASTER, *a* LACKEY.

LACKEY. Sir, your fencing master is here.

M. JOURDAIN. Bid him come in that he may give me a lesson. [*To the* MUSIC *and* DANCING MASTERS] I'd have you stay and see me perform.

Scene III.

M. JOURDAIN, FENCING MASTER, MUSIC MASTER,
DANCING MASTER, *a* LACKEY (*holding two foils*).

FENDING MASTER.   [*Taking the two foils out of the* LACKEY's *hand, and giving one to* M. JOURDAIN] Come, sir, your salute. Your body straight. A little bearing upon the left thigh. Your legs not so much a-straddle. Your feet both on a line. Your wrist opposite to your hip. The point of your sword over-against your shoulder. Your arm not quite so much extended. Your left hand on a level with your eye. Your left shoulder more square. Hold up your head. Your look bold. Advance. Your body steady. Beat carte, and push carte. One, two. Recover. Again with it, your foot firm. One, two. Leap back. When you make a pass, sir, 'tis necessary your sword should disengage first, and your body make as small a mark as possible. One, two. Come, beat tierce, and push the same. Advance. Your body firm. Advance. Quit after that manner. One, two. Recover. Repeat the same. One, two. Leap back. Parry, sir, parry. [*The* FENCING MASTER *gives him two or three home-thrusts, crying,* "*Parry*"]

M. JOURDAIN.   Ugh!

MUSIC MASTER.   You do wonders.

FENCING MASTER.   I have told you already—the whole secret of arms consists but in two things, in giving and not receiving. And as I showed you t'other day by demonstrative reason, it is impossible you should receive if you know how to turn your adversary's sword from the line of your body; which depends only upon a small motion of your wrist, either inward, or outward.

M. JOURDAIN.   At that rate therefore, a man without any courage is sure to kill his man and not to be killed.

FENCING MASTER.   Certainly. Don't you see the demonstration of it?

M. JOURDAIN.   Yes.

FENCING MASTER.   By this one may see of what consideration such persons as we should be esteemed in a state, and how highly the science of arms excels all the other useless sciences, such as dancing, music, and—

DANCING MASTER.   Soft and fair, Monsieur *Sa, sa.* Don't speak of dancing but with respect.

MUSIC MASTER.   Pray learn to treat the excellence of music in a handsomer manner.

FENCING MASTER.   You're merry fellows, to pretend to compare your sciences with mine.

MUSIC MASTER.   Do but see the importance of the creature!

DANCING MASTER.   The droll animal there, with his leathern stomacher!

FENCING MASTER.   My little master skipper, I shall make you skip as you should do. And you, my little master scraper, I shall make you sing to some tune.

DANCING MASTER.   Monsieur Tick-tack, I shall teach you your trade.

M. JOURDAIN.   [*To the* DANCING MASTER] Are you bewitched to quarrel with him, who understands tierce and carte, who knows how to kill a man by demonstrative reason?

DANCING MASTER.   I laugh at his demonstrative reason, and his tierce and his carte.

M. JOURDAIN.   [*To the* DANCING MASTER] Softly, I say.

FENCING MASTER.   [*To the* DANCING MASTER] How? Master Impertinence!

M. JOURDAIN.   Nay, my dear fencing master!

DANCING MASTER.   [*To the* FENCING MASTER] How? You great dray-horse!

M. JOURDAIN.   Nay, my dancing master.

FENCING MASTER.   If I lay my—

M. JOURDAIN.   [*To the* FENCING MASTER] Gently.

DANCING MASTER.   If I lay my clutches on you—

M. JOURDAIN.   Easily.

FENCING MASTER.   I shall curry you with such an air—

M. JOURDAIN.   [*To the* FENCING MASTER] For goodness' sake.

DANCING MASTER.   I shall drub you after such a manner—

M. JOURDAIN.   [*To the* DANCING MASTER] I beseech you.

MUSIC MASTER.   Let us teach him a little how to speak.

M. JOURDAIN.   [*To the* MUSIC MASTER] Lack-a-day, be quiet.

Scene IV.

PHILOSOPHY MASTER, M. JOURDAIN, MUSIC MASTER,
DANCING MASTER, FENCING MASTER, *a* LACKEY.

M. JOURDAIN.   Hola, Monsieur Philosopher, you are come in the nick of time with your philosophy. Come, and make peace a little amongst these people here.

PHILOSOPHY MASTER.   What's to do? What's the matter, gentlemen?

M. JOURDAIN.   They have put themselves into such a passion about the preference of their professions as to call names, and would come to blows.

PHILOSOPHY MASTER.   O fie, gentlemen, what need was there of all this fury? Have you not read the learned treatise upon anger, composed by Seneca? Is there anything more base and shameful than this passion, which makes a savage beast of a man? And should not reason be master of all our commotions?

DANCING MASTER.   How, sir? Why he has just now been abusing us both, in despising dancing which is my employment, and music which is his profession.

PHILOSOPHY MASTER.   A wise man is above all foul language that can be given him, and the grand answer one should make to all affronts is moderation and patience.

FENCING MASTER.   They had both the assurance to compare their professions to mine.

PHILOSOPHY MASTER.   Should this disturb you? Men should not dispute about vainglory and rank; that which perfectly distinguishes one from another is wisdom and virtue.

DANCING MASTER.   I maintained to him that dancing was a science to which one cannot do sufficient honour.

MUSIC MASTER.   And I, that music is one of those that all ages have revered.

FENCING MASTER.   And I maintained against 'em both that the science of defence is the finest and most necessary of all sciences.

PHILOSOPHY MASTER.   And what becomes of philosophy, then? You are all three very impertinent fellows, methinks, to speak with this arrogance before me; and impudently to give the name of science to things that one ought not to honour even with the name of art, that can't be comprised but under the name of a pitiful trade of gladiator, ballad-singer, and morris-dancer.

FENCING MASTER.   Out, ye dog of a philosopher.

MUSIC MASTER.   Hence, ye scoundrel of a pedant.

DANCING MASTER.   Begone, ye arrant pedagogue. [*The* PHILOSOPHER *falls upon them, they all three lay him on.*]

PHILOSOPHY MASTER.   How? Varlets as you are—

M. JOURDAIN.   Monsieur Philosopher!

PHILOSOPHY MASTER.   Infamous dogs! Rogues! Insolent curs!

M. JOURDAIN.   Monsieur Philosopher!

FENCING MASTER.   Plague on the animal!

M. JOURDAIN.   Gentlemen!

PHILOSOPHY MASTER.   Impudent villains!

M. JOURDAIN.   Monsieur Philosopher!

DANCING MASTER.   Deuce take the pack-saddled ass!

M. JOURDAIN.   Gentlemen!

PHILOSOPHY MASTER.   Profligate vermin!

M. JOURDAIN. Monsieur Philosopher!
MUSIC MASTER. The devil take the impertinent puppy!
M. JOURDAIN. Gentlemen!
PHILOSOPHY MASTER. Knaves! Ragamuffins! Traitors! Impostors!
M. JOURDAIN. Monsieur Philosopher! Gentlemen! Monsieur Philosopher! Gentlemen! Monsieur Philosopher! [*The four masters beat each other out.*]

Scene V.

M. JOURDAIN, *a* LACKEY.

M. JOURDAIN. Nay, beat your hearts out if you will, I shall neither meddle nor make with you, I shan't spoil my gown to part you. I should be a great fool to thrust myself among them, and receive some blow that might do me a mischief.

Scene VI.

PHILOSOPHY MASTER, M. JOURDAIN, a LACKEY.

PHILOSOPHY MASTER. [*Setting his band right*] Now to our lesson.
M. JOURDAIN. Ah! Sir, I'm sorry for the blows they have given you.
PHILOSOPHY MASTER. 'Tis nothing at all. A philosopher knows how to receive things in a proper manner; and I'll compose a satire against 'em, in the manner of Juvenal, that shall cut 'em most gloriously. Let that pass. What have you a mind to learn?
M. JOURDAIN. Everything I can, for I have all the desire in the world to be a scholar, and it vexes me that my father and mother had not made me study all the sciences when I was young.
PHILOSOPHY MASTER. 'Tis a very reasonable sentiment. *Nam, sine doctrinâ vita est quasi mortis imago.* You understand that, and are acquainted with Latin, without doubt?
M. JOURDAIN. Yes; but act as if I were not acquainted with it. Explain me the meaning of that.
PHILOSOPHY MASTER. The meaning of it is, that without learning, life is as it were an image of death.
M. JOURDAIN. That same Latin's in the right.
PHILOSOPHY MASTER. Have you not some principles, some rudiments of science?
M. JOURDAIN. Oh! yes, I can read and write.
PHILOSOPHY MASTER. Where would you please to have us begin? Would you have me teach you logic?

M. JOURDAIN.   What may that same logic be?

PHILOSOPHY MASTER.   It's that which teaches us the three operations of the mind.

M. JOURDAIN.   What are those three operations of the mind?

PHILOSOPHY MASTER.   The first, the second, and the third. The first is to conceive well, by means of universals. The second, to judge well, by means of categories. The third, to draw the conclusion right, by means of figures: Barbara, Celarent, Darii, Ferio, Baralipton, etc.

M. JOURDAIN.   These words are too crabbed. This logic does not suit me by any means. Let's learn something else that's prettier.

PHILOSOPHY MASTER.   Will you learn morality?

M. JOURDAIN.   Morality?

PHILOSOPHY MASTER.   Yes.

M. JOURDAIN.   What means morality?

PHILOSOPHY MASTER.   It treats of happiness, teaches men to moderate their passions, and—

M. JOURDAIN.   No, no more of that. I'm as choleric as the devil, and there's no morality holds me; I will have my belly full of passion whenever I have a mind to it.

PHILOSOPHY MASTER.   Would you learn physics?

M. JOURDAIN.   What is it that physics treat of?

PHILOSOPHY MASTER.   Physics are what explain the principles of things natural and the properties of bodies; which discourse of the nature of elements, of metals, of minerals, of stones, of plants, and animals, and teach us the cause of all the meteors; the rainbow, *ignes fatui*, comets, lightnings, thunder, thunder-bolts, rain, snow, hail, winds, and whirlwinds.

M. JOURDAIN.   There's too much hurly-burly in this, too much confusion.

PHILOSOPHY MASTER.   What would you have me teach you then?

M. JOURDAIN.   Teach me orthography.

PHILOSOPHY MASTER.   With all my heart.

M. JOURDAIN.   Afterwards you may teach me the almanack, to know when there's a moon, and when not.

PHILOSOPHY MASTER.   Be it so. To pursue this thought of yours right and treat this matter like a philosopher, we must begin, according to the order of things, with an exact knowledge of the nature of letters and the different manner of pronouncing them. And on this head I am to tell you that letters are divided into vowels, called vowels because they express the voice: and into consonants, so called because they sound with the vowels and only mark the different articulations of the voice. There are five vowels or voices, A, E, I, O, U.

M. JOURDAIN.   I understand all that.

PHILOSOPHY MASTER. The vowel A is formed by opening the mouth very wide, A.

M. JOURDAIN. A, A. Yes.

PHILOSOPHY MASTER. The vowel E is formed by drawing the under-jaw a little nearer to the upper, A, E.

M. JOURDAIN. A, E. A, E. In troth it is. How pretty that is!

PHILOSOPHY MASTER. And the vowel I, by bringing the jaws still nearer one to the other, and stretching the two corners of the mouth towards the ears, A, E, I.

M. JOURDAIN. A, E, I, I, I, I. 'Tis true. Long live learning!

PHILOSOPHY MASTER. The vowel O is formed by re-opening the jaws and drawing the lips near at the two corners, the upper and the under, O.

M. JOURDAIN. O, O. There's nothing more just, A, E, I, O, I, O. 'Tis admirable! I, O, I, O.

PHILOSOPHY MASTER. The opening of the mouth makes exactly a little ring, which resembles an O.

M. JOURDAIN. O, O, O. You're right, O. How fine a thing it is but to know something!

PHILOSOPHY MASTER. The vowel U is formed by bringing the teeth near together without entirely joining them, and pouting out both your lips, bringing them also near together without absolutely joining 'em, U.

M. JOURDAIN. U, U. There's nothing more true, U.

PHILOSOPHY MASTER. Your two lips pout out, as if you were making faces. Whence it comes that if you would do that to anybody and make a jest of him, you need say nothing to him but U.

M. JOURDAIN. U, U. It's true. Ah! why did not I study sooner, that I might have known all this!

PHILOSOPHY MASTER. To-morrow we shall take a view of the other letters, which are the consonants.

M. JOURDAIN. Is there anything as curious in them, as in these?

PHILOSOPHY MASTER. Doubtless. The consonant D, for example, is pronounced by clapping the tip of your tongue above the upper teeth, DE.

M. JOURDAIN. DE, DE. 'Tis so. Oh! charming things! charming things!

PHILOSOPHY MASTER. The F, in leaning the upper teeth upon the lower lip, EF.

M. JOURDAIN. EF, EF. 'Tis truth. Ah! father and mother o' mine, how do I owe you a grudge!

PHILOSOPHY MASTER. And the R, in carrying the tip of the tongue up to the roof of your mouth; so that being grazed upon by the air which bursts out with a force, it yields to it, and returns always to the same part, making a kind of trill, R, ra.

M. JOURDAIN.   R, r, ra. R, r, r, r, r, ra. That's true. What a clever man are you! And how have I lost time! R, r, r, ra.

PHILOSOPHY MASTER.   I will explain to you all these curiosities to the bottom.

M. JOURDAIN.   Pray do. But now, I must commit a secret to you. I'm in love with a person of great quality, and I should be glad you would help me to write something to her in a short *billet-doux*, which I'll drop at her feet.

PHILOSOPHY MASTER.   Very well.

M. JOURDAIN.   That will be very gallant, won't it?

PHILOSOPHY MASTER.   Without doubt. Is it verse that you would write to her?

M. JOURDAIN.   No, no, none of your verse.

PHILOSOPHY MASTER.   You would only have prose?

M. JOURDAIN.   No, I would neither have verse nor prose.

PHILOSOPHY MASTER.   It must be one or t'other.

M. JOURDAIN.   Why so?

PHILOSOPHY MASTER.   Because, sir, there's nothing to express one's self by, but prose, or verse.

M. JOURDAIN.   Is there nothing then but prose, or verse?

PHILOSOPHY MASTER.   No, sir, whatever is not prose, is verse; and whatever is not verse, is prose.

M. JOURDAIN.   And when one talks, what may that be then?

PHILOSOPHY MASTER.   Prose.

M. JOURDAIN.   How? When I say, Nicole, bring me my slippers, and give me my nightcap, is that prose?

PHILOSOPHY MASTER.   Yes, sir.

M. JOURDAIN.   On my conscience, I have spoken prose above these forty years without knowing anything of the matter; and I have all the obligations in the world to you for informing me of this. I would therefore put into a letter to her: Beautiful marchioness, your fair eyes make me die with love; but I would have this placed in a gallant manner; and have a gentle turn.

PHILOSOPHY MASTER.   Why, add that the fire of her eyes has reduced your heart to ashes: that you suffer for her night and day all the torments—

M. JOURDAIN.   No, no, no, I won't have all that—I'll have nothing but what I told you. Beautiful marchioness, your fair eyes make me die with love.

PHILOSOPHY MASTER.   You must by all means lengthen the thing out a little.

M. JOURDAIN.   No, I tell you, I'll have none but those very words in the letter: but turned in a modish way, ranged handsomely as they should be. I desire you'd show me a little, that I may see the different manners in which one may place them.

PHILOSOPHY MASTER.   One may place them first of all as you said: Beautiful marchioness, your fair eyes make me die for love. Or suppose: For love die me make, beautiful marchioness, your fair eyes. Or perhaps: Your eyes fair, for love me make, beautiful marchioness, die. Or suppose: Die your fair eyes, beautiful marchioness, for love me make. Or however: Me make your eyes fair die, beautiful marchioness, for love.

M. JOURDAIN.   But of all these ways, which is the best?

PHILOSOPHY MASTER.   That which you said: Beautiful marchioness, your fair eyes make me die for love.

M. JOURDAIN.   Yet at the same time, I never studied it, and I made the whole of it at the first touch. I thank you with all my heart, and desire you would come in good time to-morrow.

PHILOSOPHY MASTER.   I shall not fail. [*Exit*]

Scene VII.

M. JOURDAIN, *a* LACKEY.

M. JOURDAIN.   [*To his* LACKEY] What? Are my clothes not come yet?

LACKEY.   No, sir.

M. JOURDAIN.   This cursed tailor makes me wait unreasonably, considering it's a day I have so much business in. I shall go mad. A quartan ague wring this villain of a tailor. D—l take the tailor. A plague choke the tailor. If I had him but here now, this detestable tailor, this dog of a tailor, this traitor of a tailor, I—

Scene VIII.

M. JOURDAIN, MASTER TAILOR, JOURNEYMAN TAILOR (*bringing a suit of clothes for* M. JOURDAIN), *a* LACKEY.

M. JOURDAIN.   Oh! You're there. I was going to be in a passion with you.

MASTER TAILOR.   I could not possibly come sooner, and I set twenty fellows to work at your clothes.

M. JOURDAIN.   You have sent me a pair of silk hose so tight that I had all the difficulty in the world to get 'em on, and there are two stitches broke in 'em.

MASTER TAILOR.   They'll grow rather too large.

M. JOURDAIN.   Yes, if I break every day a loop or two. You have made me a pair of shoes too, that pinch me execrably.

MASTER TAILOR.   Not at all, sir.

M. JOURDAIN.   How, not at all?

MASTER TAILOR.   No, they don't pinch you at all.

M. JOURDAIN.   I tell you they do hurt me.

MASTER TAILOR.   You fancy so.

M. JOURDAIN.   I fancy so because I feel it. There's a fine reason indeed.

MASTER TAILOR.   Hold, stay, here's one of the handsomest suits at court, and the best-matched. 'Tis a masterly work to invent a grave suit of clothes that should not be black, and I'll give the cleverest tailor in town six trials to equal it.

M. JOURDAIN.   What a deuce have we here? You have put the flowers downwards.

MASTER TAILOR.   Why, you did not tell me you would have 'em upwards.

M. JOURDAIN.   Was there any need to tell you of that?

MASTER TAILOR.   Yes, certainly. All the people of quality wear 'em in that way.

M. JOURDAIN.   Do people of quality wear the flowers downwards?

MASTER TAILOR.   Yes, sir.

M. JOURDAIN.   Oh, 'tis very well, then.

MASTER TAILOR.   If you please I'll put 'em upwards.

M. JOURDAIN.   No, no.

MASTER TAILOR.   You need only say the word.

M. JOURDAIN.   No, I tell you, you have done right. Do you think my clothes will fit me?

MASTER TAILOR.   A pretty question! I defy a painter with his pencil to draw you anything that shall fit more exact. I have a fellow at home who, for fitting a pair of breeches, is the greatest genius in the world; another who, for the cut of a doublet, is the hero of the age.

M. JOURDAIN.   Are the peruke and feather as they should be?

MASTER TAILOR.   Everything's well.

M. JOURDAIN.   [Looking earnestly at the TAILOR's clothes] Ah, hah! Monsieur Tailor, here's my stuff of the last suit you made for me. I know it very well.

MASTER TAILOR.   The stuff appeared to me so handsome, that I had a mind to cut a coat out of it for myself.

M. JOURDAIN.   Yes, but you should not have cabbaged it out of mine.

MASTER TAILOR.   Will you put on your clothes?

M. JOURDAIN.   Yes, give 'em to me.

MASTER TAILOR.   Stay; the matter must not go so. I have brought men along with me to dress you to music; these sort of suits are put on with ceremony. Soho? come in there, you.

Scene IX.

M. JOURDAIN, MASTER TAILOR,
JOURNEYMAN TAILORS (*dancing*), a LACKEY.

MASTER TAILOR.   Put on this suit of the gentleman's, in the manner you do to people of quality.

[*Two of the tailors pull off his straight breeches made for his exercises, and two others his waistcoat; then they put on his new suit to music, and* M. JOURDAIN *walks amongst them to show them his clothes to see whether they fit or no.*]

JOURNEYMAN TAILOR.   My dear gentleman, please to give the tailor's men something to drink.

M. JOURDAIN.   How do you call me?

JOURNEYMAN TAILOR.   My dear gentleman.

M. JOURDAIN.   "My dear gentleman!" See what it is to dress like people of quality. You may go clothed like a commoner all your days, and they'll never call you "my dear gentleman." [*Gives them something*] Stay, there's for "my dear gentleman."

JOURNEYMAN TAILOR.   My lord, we are infinitely obliged to you.

M. JOURDAIN.   My lord! Oh, ho! My lord! Stay, friend; "my lord" deserves something, "my lord" is none o' your pretty words. Hold, there, "my lord" gives you that.

JOURNEYMAN TAILOR.   My lord, we shall go drink your grace's health.

M. JOURDAIN.   Your grace! oh, oh, oh! stay, don't go. Your grace, to me! [*Aside*] I'faith if he goes as far as highness, he'll empty my purse. [*Aloud*] Hold, there's for "my grace."

JOURNEYMAN TAILOR.   My lord, we most humbly thank your grace for your liberality.

M. JOURDAIN.   He did very well; I was going to give him all.

Act III.

Scene I.

M. JOURDAIN *and his two* LACKEYS.

M. JOURDAIN.   Follow me, that I may go and show my clothes a little through the town; and especially take care, both of you, to walk immediately at my heels, that people may plainly see you belong to me.

LACKEYS.   Yes, sir.

M. JOURDAIN.   Call me Nicole, that I may give her some directions. You need not go—here she comes.

Scene II.

M. JOURDAIN, NICOLE, *two* LACKEYS.

M. JOURDAIN.   Nicole?

NICOLE.   Your pleasure, sir?

M. JOURDAIN.   Harkee.

NICOLE.   [*Laughing*] Ha, ha, ha, ha, ha.

M. JOURDAIN.   Who do ye laugh at?

NICOLE.   Ha, ha, ha, ha, ha, ha.

M. JOURDAIN.   What does this slut mean?

NICOLE.   Ha, ha, ha. How you are bedizened! Ha, ha, ha.

M. JOURDAIN.   How's that?

NICOLE.   Oh! oh! my stars! ha, ha, ha, ha, ha.

M. JOURDAIN.   What a jade is here! What! do ye make a jest of me?

NICOLE.   No, no, sir, I should be very sorry to do so. Ha, ha, ha, ha, ha, ha.

M. JOURDAIN.   I shall give ye a slap o' the chops, if you laugh any more.

NICOLE.   Sir, I cannot help it. Ha, ha, ha, ha, ha, ha.

M. JOURDAIN.   Won't ye have done?

NICOLE. Sir, I ask your pardon; but you are so comical, that I cannot hold from laughing. Ha, ha, ha.

M. JOURDAIN. Do but see the insolence!

NICOLE. You are so thoroughly droll there! Ha, ha.

M. JOURDAIN. I shall—

NICOLE. I beg you would excuse me. Ha, ha, ha, ha.

M. JOURDAIN. Hold, if you laugh again the least in the world, I protest and swear I'll give ye such a box o' the ear as ye never had in your life.

NICOLE. Well, sir, I have done; I won't laugh any more.

M. JOURDAIN. Take care you don't. You must clean out against by and by—

NICOLE. Ha, ha.

M. JOURDAIN. You must clean out as it should be—

NICOLE. Ha, ha.

M. JOURDAIN. I say, you must go clean out the hall, and—

NICOLE. Ha, ha.

M. JOURDAIN. Again?

NICOLE. [*Tumbles down with laughing*] Hold, sir, beat me rather, and let me laugh my belly-full, that will do me more good. Ha, ha, ha, ha.

M. JOURDAIN. I shall run mad!

NICOLE. For goodness' sake, sir, I beseech you let me laugh. Ha, ha, ha.

M. JOURDAIN. If I take you in hand—

NICOLE. Si-ir, I shall bu-urst, if I do—not laugh. Ha, ha, ha.

M. JOURDAIN. But did ever anybody see such a jade as that, who insolently laughs in my face, instead of receiving my orders!

NICOLE. What would you have me do, sir?

M. JOURDAIN. Why, take care to get ready my house for the company that's to come by and by.

NICOLE. [*Getting up*] Ay, i'fakins, I've no more inclination to laugh; all your company makes such a litter here that the very word's enough to put one in an ill humour.

M. JOURDAIN. What! I ought to shut my doors against all the world for your sake?

NICOLE. You ought at least to shut it against certain people.

Scene III.

MME. JOURDAIN, M. JOURDAIN, NICOLE, *two* LACKEYS.

MME. JOURDAIN. Ah, hah! Here's some new story. What means this, husband, this same equipage? D'ye despise the world, that you harness yourself out in this manner? Have you a mind to make yourself a laughing-stock wherever ye go?

M. JOURDAIN.   None but fools, wife, will laugh at me.

MME. JOURDAIN.   In truth, people have not stayed thus long to laugh; 'tis a good while ago that your ways have furnished all the world with a laugh.

M. JOURDAIN.   Who is that "all the world," pray?

MME. JOURDAIN.   That "all the world" is a world perfectly in the right, and much wiser than yourself. For my part, I am shocked at the life you lead. I don't know what to call our house. One would swear 'twere carnival here all the year round; and from break o'day, for fear there should be any respite, there's nothing to be heard here but an uproar of fiddles and songsters which disturb the whole neighbourhood.

NICOLE.   Madame says right. I shall never see my things set to rights again for that gang of folks that you bring to the house. They ransack every quarter of the town with their feet for dirt to bring here; and poor Frances is e'en almost slaved off her legs with scrubbing of the floors, which your pretty masters come to daub as regularly as the day comes.

M. JOURDAIN.   Hey-day! our maid Nicole! you have a pretty nimble tongue of your own for a country-wench.

MME. JOURDAIN.   Nicole's in the right, and she has more sense than you have. I should be glad to know what you think to do with a dancing master, at your age?

NICOLE.   And with a lubberly fencing master, that comes here with his stamping to shake the whole house, and tear up all the pavement of the hall.

M. JOURDAIN.   Peace, our maid, and our wife.

MME. JOURDAIN.   What! will you learn to dance against the time you'll have no legs?

NICOLE.   What! have you a mind to murder somebody?

M. JOURDAIN.   Hold your prate; I tell you you are ignorant creatures, both of you, and don't know the advantage of all this.

MME. JOURDAIN.   You ought much rather to think of marrying your daughter, who is of age to be provided for.

M. JOURDAIN.   I shall think of marrying my daughter when a suitable match presents itself; but I shall think too of learning the *belles sciences*.

NICOLE.   I've heard say further, madame, that to pin the basket, he has got him a philosophy master to-day.

M. JOURDAIN.   Very well. I've a mind to have wit, and to know how to reason upon things with your genteel people.

MME. JOURDAIN.   Won't you go to school one of these days, and be whipped at your age?

M. JOURDAIN.   Why not? Would I were whipped this very instant before all the world, so I did but know what they learn at school!

NICOLE.   Yes, forsooth, that would be a mighty advantage t'ye.

M. JOURDAIN.   Without doubt.

MME. JOURDAIN.   This is all very necessary to the management of your house.

M. JOURDAIN.   Certainly. You talk, both of you, like asses, and I'm ashamed of your ignorance. [*To* MME. JOURDAIN] For example, do you know, you, what it is you now speak?

MME. JOURDAIN.   Yes, I know that what I speak is very right, and that you ought to think of living in another manner.

M. JOURDAIN.   I don't talk of that. I ask you what the words are that you now speak?

MME. JOURDAIN.   They are words that have a good deal of sense in them, and your conduct is by no means such.

M. JOURDAIN.   I don't talk of that, I tell you. I ask you, what is that I now speak to you, which I say this very moment.

MME. JOURDAIN.   Mere stuff.

M. JOURDAIN.   Pshaw, no, 'tis not that. That which we both of us say, the language we speak this instant?

MME. JOURDAIN.   Well?

M. JOURDAIN.   How is it called?

MME. JOURDAIN.   'Tis called just what you please to call it.

M. JOURDAIN.   'Tis prose, you ignorant creature.

MME. JOURDAIN.   Prose?

M. JOURDAIN.   Yes, prose. Whatever is prose, is not verse; and whatever is not verse, is prose. Now, see what it is to study. And you, [*To* NICOLE] do you know very well how you must do to say U?

NICOLE.   How?

M. JOURDAIN.   Yes. What is it you do when you say U?

NICOLE.   What?

M. JOURDAIN.   Say U a little, to try.

NICOLE.   Well, U.

M. JOURDAIN.   What is it you do?

NICOLE.   I say U.

M. JOURDAIN.   Yes, but when you say U, what is it you do?

NICOLE.   I do as you bid me.

M. JOURDAIN.   O! what a strange thing it is to have to do with brutes! You pout out your lips, and bring your under-jaw to your upper, U, d'ye see? I make a mouth, U.

NICOLE.   Yes, that's fine.

MME. JOURDAIN.   'Tis admirable!

M. JOURDAIN.   'Tis quite another thing, had but you seen O, and DE, DE, and EF, EF.

MME. JOURDAIN.   What is all this ridiculous stuff?

NICOLE.   What are we the better for all this?

M. JOURDAIN.   It makes one mad, to see these ignorant women.

MME. JOURDAIN.   Go, go, you should send all these folks apacking with their silly stuff.

NICOLE.   And especially that great lubberly fencing master, who fills all my house with dust.

M. JOURDAIN.   Hey-day! This fencing master sticks strangely in thy stomach. I'll let thee see thy impertinence presently. [*He orders the foils to be brought, and gives one to* NICOLE] Stay, reason demonstrative, the line of the body. When they push in carte one need only do so; and when they push in tierce one need only do so. This is the way never to be killed; and is not that clever to be upon sure grounds, when one has an encounter with anybody? There, push at me a little, to try.

NICOLE.   Well, how? [NICOLE *gives him several thrusts*]

M. JOURDAIN.   Gently! Hold! Oh! Softly; deuce take the hussy.

NICOLE.   You bid me push.

M. JOURDAIN.   Yes, but you push me in tierce before you push in carte, and you have not patience while I parry.

MME. JOURDAIN.   You are a fool, husband, with all these whims, and this is come to you since you have taken upon you to keep company with quality.

M. JOURDAIN.   When I keep company with quality, I show my judgment; and that's much better than herding with your bourgeoisie.

MME. JOURDAIN.   Yes, truly, there's a great deal to be got by frequenting your nobility; and you have made fine work with that count you are so bewitched with.

M. JOURDAIN.   Peace, take care what you say. Do you well know, wife, that you don't know whom you speak of when you speak of him? He's a man of more importance than you think of; a nobleman of consideration at court, who speaks to the king just for all the world as I speak to you. Is it not a thing that does me great honour, that you see a person of that quality come so often to my house, who calls me his dear friend and treats me as if I were his equal? He has more kindness for me than one would ever imagine, and he caresses me in such a manner before all the world that I myself am perfectly confounded at it.

MME. JOURDAIN.   Yes, he has a great kindness for you, and caresses you; but he borrows your money of you.

M. JOURDAIN.   Well, and is it not a great honour to me to lend

money to a man of that condition? And can I do less for a lord who calls
me his dear friend?

MME. JOURDAIN.   And what is it this lord does for you?

M. JOURDAIN.   Things that would astonish you if you did but know
'em.

MME. JOURDAIN.   And what may they be?

M. JOURDAIN.   Peace, I can't explain myself. 'Tis sufficient that if I
have lent him money, he'll pay it me honestly, and that before 'tis long.

MME. JOURDAIN.   Yes, stay you for that.

M. JOURDAIN.   Certainly. Did he not tell me so?

MME. JOURDAIN.   Yes, yes, and he won't fail to disappoint you.

M. JOURDAIN.   He swore to me on the faith of a gentleman.

MME. JOURDAIN.   A mere song.

M. JOURDAIN.   Hey! You are mighty obstinate, wife of mine; I tell
you he will keep his word with me, I am sure of it.

MME. JOURDAIN.   And I am sure that he will not, and all the court
he makes to you is only to cajole you.

M. JOURDAIN.   Hold your tongue. Here he comes.

MME. JOURDAIN.   That's all we shall have of him. He comes perhaps to borrow something more of you; the very sight of him gives me
my dinner.

M. JOURDAIN.   Hold your tongue, I say.

Scene IV.

DORANTE, M. JOURDAIN, MME. JOURDAIN, NICOLE.

DORANTE.   My dear friend, Monsieur Jourdain, how do you do?

M. JOURDAIN.   Very well, sir, to do you what little service I can.

DORANTE.   And Madame Jourdain there, how does she do?

MME. JOURDAIN.   Madame Jourdain does as well as she can.

DORANTE.   Hah! Monsieur Jourdain, you're dressed the most gen-
teelly in the world!

M. JOURDAIN.   As you see.

DORANTE.   You have a very fine air with that dress, and we have
ne'er a young fellow at court that's better made than you.

M. JOURDAIN.   He, he.

MME. JOURDAIN.   [*Aside*] He scratches him where it itches.

DORANTE.   Turn about. 'Tis most gallant.

MME. JOURDAIN.   [*Aside*] Yes, as much of the fool behind as before.

DORANTE.   'Faith, Monsieur Jourdain, I was strangely impatient to
see you. You're the man in the world I most esteem, and I was talking
of you again this morning at the king's levee.

M. JOURDAIN.   You do me a great deal of honour, sir. [*To* MME. JOURDAIN] At the king's levee!

DORANTE.   Come, be covered.

M. JOURDAIN.   Sir, I know the respect I owe you.

DORANTE.   Lack-a-day, be covered; no ceremony, pray, between us two.

M. JOURDAIN.   Sir—

DORANTE.   Put on your hat, I tell you, Monsieur Jourdain; you are my friend.

M. JOURDAIN.   Sir, I am your humble servant.

DORANTE.   I won't be covered, if you won't.

M. JOURDAIN.   [*Puts on his hat*] I choose rather to be unmannerly than troublesome.

DORANTE.   I am your debtor, you know.

MME. JOURDAIN.   [*Aside*] Yes, we know it but too well.

DORANTE.   You have generously lent me money upon several occasions; and have obliged me, most certainly, with the best grace in the world.

M. JOURDAIN.   You jest, sir.

DORANTE.   But I know how to repay what is lent me, and to be grateful for the favours done me.

M. JOURDAIN.   I don't doubt it, sir.

DORANTE.   I'm willing to get out of your books, and came hither to make up our accounts together.

M. JOURDAIN.   [*Aside to* MME. JOURDAIN] Well, you see your impertinence, wife.

DORANTE.   I'm one who love to be out of debt as soon as I can.

M. JOURDAIN.   [*Aside to* MME. JOURDAIN] I told you so.

DORANTE.   Let's see a little what 'tis I owe you.

M. JOURDAIN.   [*Aside to* MME. JOURDAIN] You there, with your ridiculous suspicions.

DORANTE.   Do you remember right all the money you have lent me?

M. JOURDAIN.   I believe so. I made a little memorandum of it. Here it is. Let you have at one time two hundred louis d'or.

DORANTE.   'Tis true.

M. JOURDAIN.   Another time, six-score.

DORANTE.   Yes.

M. JOURDAIN.   And another time a hundred and forty.

DORANTE.   You are right.

M. JOURDAIN.   These three articles make four hundred and sixty louis d'or, which come to five thousand and sixty livres.

DORANTE.   The account is very right. Five thousand and sixty livres.

M. JOURDAIN.   One thousand eight hundred and thirty-two livres to your plume-maker.

DORANTE.   Just.

M. JOURDAIN.   Two thousand seven hundred and four-score livres to your tailor.

DORANTE.   'Tis true.

M. JOURDAIN.   Four thousand three hundred and seventy-nine livres, twelve sols, and eight deniers to your tradesman.

DORANTE.   Very well. Twelve sols, eight deniers. The account is just.

M. JOURDAIN.   And a thousand seven hundred and forty-eight livres, seven sols, four deniers to your saddler.

DORANTE.   'Tis all true. What does that come to?

M. JOURDAIN.   Sum total, fifteen thousand eight hundred livres.

DORANTE.   The sum total, and just. Fifteen thousand and eight hundred livres. To which add two hundred pistoles, which you are going to lend me, that will make exactly eighteen thousand francs, which I shall pay you the first opportunity.

MME. JOURDAIN.   [*Aside to* M. JOURDAIN] Well, did I not guess how 'twould be!

M. JOURDAIN.   [*Aside to* MME. JOURDAIN] Peace.

DORANTE.   Will it incommode you to lend me what I tell you?

M. JOURDAIN.   Oh! no.

MME. JOURDAIN.   [*Aside to* M. JOURDAIN] This man makes a mere milch cow of you.

M. JOURDAIN.   [*Aside to* MME. JOURDAIN] Hold your tongue.

DORANTE.   If this will incommode you, I'll seek it elsewhere.

M. JOURDAIN.   No, sir.

MME. JOURDAIN.   [*Aside to* M. JOURDAIN] He'll ne'er be satisfied till he has ruined you.

M. JOURDAIN.   [*Aside to* MME. JOURDAIN] Hold your tongue, I tell you.

DORANTE.   You need only tell me if this puts you to any straits.

M. JOURDAIN.   Not at all, sir.

MME. JOURDAIN.   [*Aside to* M. JOURDAIN] 'Tis a true wheedler.

M. JOURDAIN.   [*Aside to* MME. JOURDAIN] Hold your tongue then.

MME. JOURDAIN.   [*Aside to* M. JOURDAIN] He'll drain you to the last farthing.

M. JOURDAIN.   [*Aside to* MME. JOURDAIN] Will you hold your tongue?

DORANTE.   I've a good many people would be glad to lend it me, but as you are my very good friend, I thought I should wrong you if I asked it of anybody else.

M. JOURDAIN.   'Tis too much honour, sir, you do me. I'll go fetch
what you want.

MME. JOURDAIN.   [*Aside to* M. JOURDAIN] What! going to lend him
still more?

M. JOURDAIN.   [*Aside to* MME. JOURDAIN] What can I do? Would
you have me refuse a man of that rank, who spoke of me this morning
at the king's levee?

MME. JOURDAIN.   [*Aside to* M. JOURDAIN] Go, you're a downright
dupe.

Scene V.

DORANTE, MME. JOURDAIN, NICOLE.

DORANTE.   You seem to me very melancholy. What ails you,
Madame Jourdain?

MME. JOURDAIN.   My head's bigger than my fist, even if it is not
swelled.

DORANTE.   Where is Mademoiselle your daughter that I don't see
her?

MME. JOURDAIN.   Mademoiselle my daughter is pretty well where
she is.

DORANTE.   How does she go on?

MME. JOURDAIN.   She goes on her two legs.

DORANTE.   Won't you come with her, one of these days, and see the
ball, and the play that's acted at court?

MME. JOURDAIN.   Yes, truly, we've a great inclination to laugh, a
great inclination to laugh have we.

DORANTE.   I fancy, Madame Jourdain, you had a great many sparks
in your younger years, being so handsome and good-humoured as you
were.

MME. JOURDAIN.   Tredame, sir! what, is Madame Jourdain grown
decrepit, and does her head totter already with a palsy?

DORANTE.   Odso, Madame Jourdain, I ask your pardon. I was not
thinking that you are young. I'm very often absent. Pray excuse my impertinence.

Scene VI.

M. JOURDAIN, MME. JOURDAIN, DORANTE, NICOLE.

M. JOURDAIN.   [*To* DORANTE] Here's two hundred pieces for you,
hard money.

DORANTE.   I do assure you, Monsieur Jourdain, I am absolutely yours; and I long to do you service at court.

M. JOURDAIN.   I'm infinitely obliged to you.

DORANTE.   If Madame Jourdain inclines to see the royal diversion, I'll get her the best places in the ballroom.

MME. JOURDAIN.   Madame Jourdain kisses your hand.

DORANTE.   [*Aside to* M. JOURDAIN] Our pretty marchioness, as I informed you in my letter, will be here by and by to partake of your ball and collation; I brought her, at last, to consent to the entertainment you design to give her.

M. JOURDAIN.   Let us draw to a distance a little, for a certain reason.

DORANTE.   'Tis eight days since I saw you, and I gave you no tidings of the diamond you put into my hands to make her a present of, as from you; but the reason was, I had all the difficulty in the world to conquer her scruples, and 'twas no longer ago than to-day, that she resolved to accept of it.

M. JOURDAIN.   How did she like it?

DORANTE.   Marvellously; and I am much deceived if the beauty of this diamond has not an admirable effect upon her.

M. JOURDAIN.   Grant it, kind Heaven!

MME. JOURDAIN.   [*To* NICOLE] When he's once with him, he can never get rid of him.

DORANTE.   I made her sensible in a proper manner of the richness of the present and the strength of your passion.

M. JOURDAIN.   These kindnesses perfectly overwhelm me; I am in the greatest confusion in the world to see a person of your quality demean himself on my account as you do.

DORANTE.   You jest sure. Does one ever stop at such sort of scruples among friends? And would not you do the same thing for me, if occasion offered?

M. JOURDAIN.   Oh! certainly, and with all my soul.

MME. JOURDAIN.   [*Aside to* NICOLE] How the sight of him torments me!

DORANTE.   For my part, I never mind anything when a friend is to be served; and when you imparted to me the ardent passion you had entertained for the agreeable marchioness, with whom I was acquainted, you see that I made an immediate offer of my service.

M. JOURDAIN.   'Tis true, these favours are what confound me.

MME. JOURDAIN.   [*To* NICOLE] What! will he never be gone?

NICOLE.   They are mighty great together.

DORANTE.   You've taken the right way to smite her. Women, above all things, love the expense we are at on their account; and your frequent serenades, your continual entertainments, that sumptuous firework she saw on the water, the diamond she received by way of present from you, and the regale you are now preparing—all this speaks much better in favour of your passion than all the things you yourself could possibly have said to her.

M. JOURDAIN.   There's no expense I would not be at, if I could by that means find the way to her heart. A woman of quality has powerful charms for me, and 'tis an honour I would purchase at any rate.

MME. JOURDAIN.   [*Aside to* NICOLE] What can they have to talk of so long together? Go softly, and listen a little.

DORANTE.   By and by you will enjoy the pleasure of seeing her at your ease; your eyes will have full time to be satisfied.

M. JOURDAIN.   To be at full liberty, I have ordered matters so that my wife shall dine with my sister, where she'll pass the whole afternoon.

DORANTE.   You have done wisely, for your wife might have perplexed us a little. I have given the proper orders for you to the cook, and for everything necessary for the ball. 'Tis of my own invention; and provided the execution answers the plan, I am sure 'twill be—

M. JOURDAIN.   [*Perceives that* NICOLE *listens, and gives her a box on the ear*] Hey, you're very impertinent. [*To* DORANTE] Let us go if you please.

Scene VII.

MME. JOURDAIN, NICOLE.

NICOLE.   I'faith, curiosity has cost me something; but I believe there's a snake in the grass, for they were talking of some affair which they were not willing you should be present at.

MME. JOURDAIN.   This is not the first time, Nicole, that I have had suspicions of my husband. I am the most deceived person in the world, or there is some amour in agitation, and I am labouring to discover what it should be. But let's think of my daughter. You know the love Cléonte has for her. He is a man who hits my fancy, and I have a mind to favour his addresses and help him to Lucile, if I can.

NICOLE.   In truth, madame, I am the most ravished creature in the world, to find you in these sentiments; for if the master hits your taste, the man hits mine no less; and I could wish our marriage might be concluded under favour of theirs.

MME. JOURDAIN.   Go, and talk with him about it, as from me, and tell him to come to me presently, that we may join in demanding my daughter of my husband.

NICOLE.   I fly, madame, with joy, and I could not have received a more agreeable commission. [*Alone*] I believe I shall very much rejoice their hearts.

Scene VIII.

CLÉONTE, COVIELLE, NICOLE.

NICOLE. Hah, most luckily met. I'm an ambassadress of joy, and I come—

CLÉONTE. Be gone, ye perfidious slut, and don't come to amuse me with thy traitorous speeches.

NICOLE. Is it thus you receive—

CLÉONTE. Be gone, I tell thee, and go directly and inform thy false mistress, that she never more, while she lives, shall impose upon the too simple Cléonte.

NICOLE. What whim is this? My dear Covielle, tell me a little what does this mean.

COVIELLE. Thy dear Covielle, wicked minx? Away quickly out of my sight, hussy, and leave me at quiet.

NICOLE. What! dost thou, too—

COVIELLE. Out o' my sight, I tell thee, and talk not to me, for thy life.

NICOLE. [*Aside*] Hey-day! What gadfly has stung 'em both? Well, I must march and inform my mistress of this pretty piece of history.

Scene IX.

CLÉONTE, COVIELLE.

CLÉONTE. What! treat a lover in this manner; and a lover the most constant, the most passionate of all lovers!

COVIELLE. 'Tis a horrible trick they have served us both.

CLÉONTE. I discover all the ardour for her, all the tenderness one can imagine. I love nothing in the world but her, have nothing in my thoughts besides her. She is all my care, all my desire, all my joy. I speak of nought but her, think of nought but her, dream of nought but her, I breathe only for her, my heart lives wholly in her; and this is the worthy recompense of such a love! I am two days without seeing her, which are to me two horrible ages; I meet her accidentally, my heart feels all transported at the sight; joy sparkles in my face; I fly to her with ecstasy, and the faithless creature turns away her eyes, and brushes hastily by me, as if she had never seen me in her life!

COVIELLE. I say the same as you do.

CLÉONTE. Is it possible to see anything, Covielle, equal to this perfidy of the ungrateful Lucile?

COVIELLE. Or to that, sir, of the villainous jade Nicole?

CLÉONTE.   After so many ardent sacrifices of sighs and vows that I have made to her charms!

COVIELLE.   After so much assiduous sneaking, cares, and services that I have paid her in the kitchen!

CLÉONTE.   So many tears that I have shed at her feet!

COVIELLE.   So many buckets of water that I have drawn for her!

CLÉONTE.   Such ardour as I have shown, in loving her more than myself!

COVIELLE.   So much heat as I have endured, in turning the spit in her place!

CLÉONTE.   She flies me with disdain!

COVIELLE.   She turns her back upon me with impudence!

CLÉONTE.   This is a perfidy worthy the greatest punishment.

COVIELLE.   This a treachery that deserves a thousand boxes o' the ear.

CLÉONTE.   Prithee, never think to speak once more to me in her favour.

COVIELLE.   I, sir? Marry, Heaven forbid.

CLÉONTE.   Never come to excuse the action of this perfidious woman.

COVIELLE.   Fear it not.

CLÉONTE.   No, d'ye see, all discourses in her defence will signify nothing.

COVIELLE.   Who dreams of such a thing?

CLÉONTE.   I'm determined to continue my resentment against her, and break off all correspondence.

COVIELLE.   I give my consent.

CLÉONTE.   This same count that visits her, pleases perhaps her eye; and her fancy, I see plainly, is dazzled with quality. But I must, for my own honour, prevent the triumph of her inconstancy. I'll make as much haste as she can do towards the change which I see she's running into, and won't leave her all the glory of quitting me.

COVIELLE.   'Tis very well said, and for my share, I enter into all your sentiments.

CLÉONTE.   Second my resentments, and support my resolutions against all the remains of love that may yet plead for her. I conjure thee, say all the ill things of her thou canst. Paint me her person so as to make her despicable; and, in order to disgust me, mark me out well all the faults thou canst find in her.

COVIELLE.   She, sir? A pretty mawkin, a fine piece to be so much enamoured with. I see nothing in her but what's very indifferent, and you might find a hundred persons more deserving of you. First of all she has little eyes.

CLÉONTE.   That's true, she has little eyes; but they are full of fire, the most sparkling, the most piercing in the world, the most striking that one shall see.

COVIELLE.   She has a wide mouth.

CLÉONTE.   Yes; but one sees such graces in it, as one does not see in other mouths, and the sight of that mouth inspires desire: 'tis the most attractive, the most amorous in the world.

COVIELLE.   As to her height, she's not tall.

CLÉONTE.   No; but she's easy, and well-shaped.

COVIELLE.   She affects a negligence in speaking and acting.

CLÉONTE.   'Tis true; but all this has a gracefulness in her, and her ways are engaging; they have I don't know what charms that insinuate into our hearts.

COVIELLE.   As to her wit—

CLÉONTE.   Ah! Covielle, she has the most refined, the most delicate turn of wit.

COVIELLE.   Her conversation—

CLÉONTE.   Her conversation is charming.

COVIELLE.   She's always grave.

CLÉONTE.   Would you have flaunting pleasantry, a perpetual profuse mirth? And d'ye see anything more impertinent than those women who are always upon the giggle?

COVIELLE.   But in short, she is the most capricious creature in the world.

CLÉONTE.   Yes, she is capricious, I grant ye, but everything sits well upon fine women; we bear with everything from the fair.

COVIELLE.   Since that's the case, I see plainly you desire always to love her.

CLÉONTE.   I! I should love death sooner; and I am now going to hate her as much as ever I loved her.

COVIELLE.   But how, if you think her so perfect?

CLÉONTE.   Therein shall my vengeance be more glaring; therein shall I better display the force of my resolution in hating her, quitting her, most beautiful as she is; most charming, most amiable, as I think her. Here she is.

Scene X.

LUCILE, CLÉONTE, COVIELLE, NICOLE.

NICOLE.   [*To* LUCILE] For my part, I was perfectly shocked at it.

LUCILE.   It can be nothing else, Nicole, but what I said. But there he comes.

CLÉONTE.   [*To* COVIELLE] I won't so much as speak to her.

COVIELLE.   I'll follow your example.

LUCILE.   What means this, Cléonte, what's the matter with you?

NICOLE.   What ails thee, Covielle?

LUCILE.   What trouble has seized you?

NICOLE.   What cross humour possesses thee?

LUCILE.   Are you dumb, Cléonte?

NICOLE.   Hast thou lost thy speech, Covielle?

CLÉONTE.   The abandoned creature!

COVIELLE.   Oh! the Judas!

LUCILE.   I see very well that the late meeting has disordered your mind.

CLÉONTE.   [*To* COVIELLE] O, ho! She sees what she has done.

NICOLE.   The reception of this morning has made thee take snuff.

COVIELLE.   [*To* CLÉONTE] She has guessed where the shoe pinches.

LUCILE.   Is it not true, Cléonte, that this is the reason of your being out of humour?

CLÉONTE.   Yes, perfidious maid, that is it, since I must speak; and I can tell you that you shall not triumph, as you imagine, by your unfaithfulness, that I shall be beforehand in breaking with you, and you won't have the credit of discarding me. I shall, doubtless, have some difficulty in conquering the passion I have for you: 'twill cause me uneasiness; I shall suffer for a while; but I shall compass my point, and I would sooner stab myself to the heart than have the weakness of returning to you.

COVIELLE.   [*To* NICOLE] As says the master, so says the man.

LUCILE.   Here's a noise indeed about nothing. I'll tell you, Cléonte, the reason that made me avoid joining you this morning.

CLÉONTE.   [*Endeavouring to go to avoid* LUCILE] No, I'll hear nothing.

NICOLE.   [*To* COVIELLE] I'll let thee into the cause that made us pass you so quick.

COVIELLE.   [*Endeavouring to go to avoid* NICOLE] I will hear nothing.

LUCILE.   [*Following* CLÉONTE] Know that this morning—

CLÉONTE.   [*Walks about without regarding* LUCILE] No, I tell you.

NICOLE.   [*Following* COVIELLE] Learn that—

COVIELLE.   [*Walks about likewise without regarding* NICOLE] No, traitress.

LUCILE.   Hear me.

CLÉONTE.   Not a bit.

NICOLE.   Let me speak.

COVIELLE. I'm deaf.

LUCILE. Cléonte!

CLÉONTE. No.

NICOLE. Covielle!

COVIELLE. No.

LUCILE. Stay.

CLÉONTE. Idle stuff.

NICOLE. Hear me.

COVIELLE. No such thing.

LUCILE. One moment.

CLÉONTE. Not at all.

NICOLE. A little patience.

COVIELLE. A fiddle-stick.

LUCILE. Two words.

CLÉONTE. No, 'tis over.

NICOLE. One word.

COVIELLE. No more dealings.

LUCILE. [*Stopping*] Well, since you won't hear me, keep your opinion, and do what you please.

NICOLE. [*Stopping likewise*] Since that's thy way, e'en take it all just as it pleases thee.

CLÉONTE. Let's know the subject then of this fine reception.

LUCILE. [*Going in her turn to avoid* CLÉONTE] I've no longer an inclination to tell it.

COVIELLE. Let us a little into this history.

NICOLE. [*Going likewise in her turn to avoid* COVIELLE] I won't inform thee now, not I.

CLÉONTE. [*Following* LUCILE] Tell me—

LUCILE. No, I'll tell you nothing.

COVIELLE. [*Following* NICOLE] Say—

NICOLE. No, I say nothing.

CLÉONTE. For goodness' sake.

LUCILE. No, I tell you.

COVIELLE. Of all charity.

NICOLE. Not a bit.

CLÉONTE. I beseech you.

LUCILE. Let me alone.

COVIELLE. I conjure thee.

NICOLE. Away with thee.

CLÉONTE. Lucile!

LUCILE. No.

COVIELLE. Nicole!

NICOLE. Not at all.

CLÉONTE.   For Heaven's sake.

LUCILE.   I will not.

COVIELLE.   Speak to me.

NICOLE.   Not a word.

CLÉONTE.   Clear up my doubts.

LUCILE.   No, I'll do nothing towards it.

COVIELLE.   Cure my mind.

NICOLE.   No, 'tis not my pleasure.

CLÉONTE.   Well, since you are so little concerned to ease me of my pain, and to justify yourself as to the unworthy treatment my passion has received from you, ungrateful creature, 'tis the last time you shall see me, and I am going far from you to die of grief and love.

COVIELLE.   [To NICOLE] And I'll follow his steps.

LUCILE.   [To CLÉONTE, *who is going*] Cléonte!

NICOLE.   [To COVIELLE, *who follows his master*] Covielle!

CLÉONTE.   [*Stopping*] Hey?

COVIELLE.   [*Likewise stopping*] Your pleasure?

LUCILE.   Whither do you go?

CLÉONTE.   Where I told you.

COVIELLE.   We go to die.

LUCILE.   Do you go to die, Cléonte?

CLÉONTE.   Yes, cruel, since you will have it so.

LUCILE.   I? I have you die?

CLÉONTE.   Yes, you would.

LUCILE.   Who told you so?

CLÉONTE.   [*Going up to* LUCILE] Would you not have it so, since you would not clear up my suspicions?

LUCILE.   Is that my fault? Would you but have given me the hearing, should I not have told you that the adventure you make such complaints about was occasioned this morning by the presence of an old aunt who will absolutely have it that the mere approach of a man is a dishonour to a girl, who is perpetually lecturing us upon this head, and represents to us all mankind as so many devils, whom one ought to avoid.

NICOLE.   [To COVIELLE] There's the whole secret of the affair.

CLÉONTE.   Don't you deceive me, Lucile?

COVIELLE.   [To NICOLE] Dost thou not put a trick upon me?

LUCILE.   [To CLÉONTE] There's nothing more true.

NICOLE.   [To COVIELLE] 'Tis the very thing, as it is.

COVIELLE.   [To CLÉONTE] Shall we surrender upon this?

CLÉONTE.   Ah, Lucile, what art have you to calm my passions with a single word! How easily do we suffer ourselves to be persuaded by those we love!

COVIELLE.   How easily is one wheedled by these plaguy animals!

Scene XI.

MME. JOURDAIN, CLÉONTE, LUCILE, COVIELLE, NICOLE.

MME JOURDAIN.   I am very glad to see you, Cléonte, and you are here apropos. My husband's acoming; catch your opportunity quick, and demand Lucile in marriage.

CLÉONTE.   Ah, madame, how sweet is that word, how it flatters my wishes! Could I receive an order more charming? a favour more precious?

Scene XII.

CLÉONTE, M. JOURDAIN, MME. JOURDAIN,
LUCILE, COVIELLE, NICOLE.

CLÉONTE.   Sir, I was not willing to employ any other person to make a certain demand of you which I have long intended. It concerns me sufficiently to undertake it in my own person; and, without farther circumlocution, I shall inform you that the honour of being your son-in-law is an illustrious favour which I beseech you to grant me.

M. JOURDAIN.   Before I give you an answer, sir, I desire you would tell me whether you are a gentleman.

CLÉONTE.   Sir, the generality of people don't hesitate much on this question. People speak out bluff, and with ease. They make no scruple of taking this title upon 'em, and custom now-a-days seems to authorise the theft. For my part, I confess to you, my sentiments in this matter are somewhat more delicate. I look upon all imposture as unworthy an honest man, and that there is cowardice in denying what Heaven has made us; in tricking ourselves out, to the eyes of the world, in a stolen title; in desiring to put ourselves off for what we are not. I am undoubtedly born of parents who have held honourable employments. I have had the honour of six years' service in the army; and I find myself of consequence enough to hold a tolerable rank in the world; but for all this I won't give myself a name, which others in my place would think they might pretend to, and I'll tell you frankly that I am no gentleman.

M. JOURDAIN.   Your hand, sir; my daughter is no wife for you.

CLÉONTE.   How?

M. JOURDAIN.   You are no gentleman, you shan't have my daughter.

MME. JOURDAIN.   What would you be at then with your gentlemen? D'ye think we sort of people are of the line of St. Louis?

M. JOURDAIN.   Hold your tongue, wife, I see you're acoming.

MME. JOURDAIN.   Are we either of us otherwise descended than of plain citizens?

M. JOURDAIN.   There's a scandalous reflection for you!

MME. JOURDAIN.   And was not your father a tradesman as well as mine?

M. JOURDAIN.   Plague take the woman! She never has done with this. If your father was a tradesman, so much was the worse for him; but as for mine, they are numskulls that say he was. All that I have to say to you is that I will have a gentleman for my son-in-law.

MME. JOURDAIN.   Your daughter should have a husband that's proper for her, and an honest man who is rich and well made would be much better for her than a gentleman who is deformed and a beggar.

NICOLE.   That's very true. We have a young squire in our town who is the most awkward looby, the veriest driveller that I ever set eyes on.

M. JOURDAIN.   Hold your prate, Madame Impertinence. You are always thrusting yourself into conversation. I've means sufficient for my daughter, and want nothing but honour, and I will have her a marchioness.

MME. JOURDAIN.   A marchioness!

M. JOURDAIN.   Yes, a marchioness.

MME. JOURDAIN.   Marry, Heaven preserve me from it!

M. JOURDAIN.   'Tis a determined thing.

MME. JOURDAIN.   'Tis what I shall never consent to. Matches with people above one are always subject to grievous inconveniences. I don't like that a son-in-law should have it in his power to reproach my daughter with her parents, or that she should have children who should be ashamed to call me grandmother. Should she come and visit me with the equipage of a grand lady and, through inadvertency, miss curtsying to some of the neighbourhood, they would not fail, presently, saying a hundred idle things. Do but see, would they say, this lady marchioness, what haughty airs she gives herself! She's the daughter of Monsieur Jourdain, who was over and above happy, when she was a little one, to play children's play with us. She was not always so lofty as she is now; and her two grandfathers sold cloth near St. Innocent's Gate. They amassed great means for their children, which they are paying for now, perhaps very dear, in the other world. People don't generally grow so rich by being honest. I won't have all these tittle-tattle stories; in one word, I'll have a man who shall be beholden to me for my daughter, and to whom I can say. Sit you down there, son-in-law, and dine with me.

M. JOURDAIN.   See there the sentiments of a little soul, to desire always to continue in a mean condition. Let me have no more replies; my daughter shall be a marchioness in spite of the world; and if you put me in a passion, I'll make her a duchess.

Scene XIII.

MME. JOURDAIN, LUCILE, CLÉONTE, NICOLE, COVIELLE.

MME. JOURDAIN. Cléonte, don't be discouraged by all this. [*To* LUCILE] Follow me, daughter, and come tell your father resolutely that if you have not him, you won't marry anybody at all.

Scene XIV.

CLÉONTE, COVIELLE.

COVIELLE. You have made a pretty piece of work of it with your fine sentiments.
CLÉONTE. What wouldst thou have me do? I have a scrupulousness in this case that no precedents can conquer.
COVIELLE. You're in the wrong to be serious with such a man as that. Don't you see that he's a fool? And would it cost you anything to accommodate yourself to his chimeras?
CLÉONTE. You're in the right; but I did not dream it was necessary to bring your proofs of nobility, to be son-in-law to Monsieur Jourdain.
COVIELLE. [*Laughing*] Ha, ha, ha.
CLÉONTE. What d'ye laugh at?
COVIELLE. At a thought that's come into my head to play our spark off and help you to obtain what you desire.
CLÉONTE. How?
COVIELLE. The thought is absolutely droll.
CLÉONTE. What is it?
COVIELLE. There was a certain masquerade performed a little while ago, which comes in here the best in the world; and which I intend to insert into a piece of roguery I design to make for our coxcomb. This whole affair looks a little like making a joke of him; but with him we may hazard everything. There's no need here to study finesse so much—he's a man who will play his part to a wonder, and will easily give in to all the sham tales we shall take in our heads to tell him. I have actors, I have habits all ready, only let me alone.
CLÉONTE. But inform me of it.
COVIELLE. I am going to let you into the whole of it. Let's retire; there he comes.

Scene XV.

M. JOURDAIN (*alone*).

M. JOURDAIN.   What a deuce can this mean? They have nothing but great lords to reproach me with; and I for my part see nothing so fine as keeping company with your great lords; there's nothing but honour and civility among 'em, and I would it had cost me two fingers of a hand to have been born a count or a marquis.

Scene XVI.

M. JOURDAIN, *a* LACKEY.

LACKEY.   Sir, here's the count, and a lady whom he's handing in.
M. JOURDAIN.   Good lack-a-day, I have some orders to give. Tell 'em that I'm acoming in a minute.

Scene XVII.

DORIMÈNE, DORANTE, *a* LACKEY.

LACKEY.   My master says that he's acoming in a minute.

Scene XVIII.

DORIMÈNE, DORANTE.

DORANTE.   'Tis very well.
DORIMÈNE.   I don't know, Dorante; I take a strange step here in suffering you to bring me to a house where I know nobody.
DORANTE.   What place then, madame, would you have a lover choose to entertain you in, since, to avoid clamour, you neither allow of your own house nor mine?
DORIMÈNE.   But you don't mention that I am every day insensibly engaged to receive too great proofs of your passion. In vain do I refuse things, you weary me out of resistance, and you have a civil kind of obstinacy which makes me come gently into whatsoever you please. Frequent visits commenced, declarations came next, which drew after them serenades and entertainments, which were followed by presents. I opposed all these things, but you are not disheartened, and you become master of my resolutions step by step. For my part, I can answer for nothing hereafter, and I believe in the

end you will bring me to matrimony, from which I stood so far
aloof.

DORANTE.   Faith, madame, you ought to have been there already.
You are a widow, and depend upon nobody but yourself. I am my own
master, and love you more than my life. What does it stick at, then, that
you should not, from this day forward, complete my happiness?

DORIMÈNE.   Lack-a-day, Dorante, there must go a great many qual-
ities on both sides, to make people live happily together; and two of the
most reasonable persons in the world have often much ado to compose
a union to both their satisfactions.

DORANTE.   You're in the wrong, madame, to represent to yourself
so many difficulties in this affair; and the experience you have had con-
cludes nothing for the rest of the world.

DORIMÈNE.   In short, I always abide by this. The expenses you put
yourself to for me disturb me for two reasons; one is, they engage me
more than I could wish; and the other is, I'm sure (no offence to you!)
that you can't do this but you must incommode yourself, and I would
not have you do that.

DORANTE.   Fie, madame, these are trifles, and 'tis not by that—

DORIMÈNE.   I know what I say; and, amongst other things, the diamond you forced me to take, is of value—

DORANTE.   Nay, madame, pray don't enhance the value of a thing
my love thinks unworthy of you: and permit—Here's the master of the
house.

Scene XIX.

M. JOURDAIN, DORIMÈNE, DORANTE.

M. JOURDAIN.   [*After having made two bows, finding himself too
near* DORIMÈNE] A little farther, madame.

DORIMÈNE.   How?

M. JOURDAIN.   One step, if you please.

DORIMÈNE.   What then?

M. JOURDAIN.   Fall back a little for the third.

DORANTE.   Monsieur Jourdain, madame, knows the world.

M. JOURDAIN.   Madame, 'tis a very great honour that I am fortunate
enough to be so happy, but to have the felicity that you should have the
goodness to grant me the favour, to do me the honour, to honour me
with the favour of your presence; and had I also the merit to merit a
merit like yours, and that Heaven—envious of my good—had granted
me—the advantage of being worthy—of—

DORANTE.   Monsieur Jourdain, enough of this; my lady does not love great compliments, and she knows you are a man of wit. [*Aside to* DORIMÈNE] 'Tis a downright bourgeois, ridiculous enough, as you see, in his whole behaviour.

DORIMÈNE.   [*Aside to* DORANTE] It is not very difficult to perceive it.

DORANTE.   Madame, this is a very good friend of mine.

M. JOURDAIN.   'Tis too much honour you do me.

DORANTE.   A very polite man.

DORIMÈNE.   I have a great esteem for him.

M. JOURDAIN.   I have done nothing yet, madame, to merit this favour.

DORANTE.   [*Aside to* M. JOURDAIN] Take good care however not to speak to her of the diamond you gave her.

M. JOURDAIN.   [*Aside to* DORANTE] Mayn't I ask her only how she likes it?

DORANTE.   [*Aside to* M. JOURDAIN] How! Take special care you don't. 'Twould be villainous of you; and to act like a man of gallantry, you should make as if it were not you who made the present. [*Aloud*] Monsieur Jourdain, madame, says that he's in raptures to see you at his house.

DORIMÈNE.   He does me a great deal of honour.

M. JOURDAIN.   [*To* DORANTE] How am I obliged to you, sir, for speaking to her in that manner on my account!

DORANTE.   [*Aside to* M. JOURDAIN] I have had a most terrible difficulty to get her to come hither.

M. JOURDAIN.   [*To* DORANTE] I don't know how to thank you enough for it.

DORANTE.   He says, madame, that he thinks you the most charming person in the world.

DORIMÈNE.   'Tis a great favour he does me.

M. JOURDAIN.   Madame, it's you who do the favours, and—

DORANTE.   Let's think of eating.

Scene XX.

M. JOURDAIN, DORIMÈNE, DORANTE, *a* LACKEY.

LACKEY.   Everything is ready, sir.

DORANTE.   Come, then, let us sit down to table; and fetch the musicians.

Act IV.

Scene I.

DORIMÈNE, MONSIEUR JOURDAIN,
DORANTE, *three* MUSICIANS, LACKEYS.

DORIMÈNE.   How, Dorante? Why here's a most magnificent repast!

M. JOURDAIN.   You are pleased to banter, madame; I would it were more worthy of your acceptance. [DORIMÈNE, M. JOURDAIN, DORANTE, *and three* MUSICIANS *sit down at the table*]

DORANTE.   Monsieur Jourdain, madame, is in the right in what he says, and he obliges me in paying you, after so handsome a manner, the honours of his house. I agree with him that the repast is not worthy of you. As it was myself who ordered it, and I am not so clearly sighted in these affairs as certain of our friends, you have here no very learned feast; and you will find incongruities of good cheer in it, some barbarisms of good taste. Had our friend Damis had a hand here, everything had been done by rule; elegance and erudition would have run through the whole, and he would not have failed exaggerating all the regular pieces of the repast he gave you, and force you to own his great capacity in the science of good eating; he would have told you of bread *de rive*, with the golden kissing-crust, raised too all round with a crust that crumples tenderly in your teeth; of wine with a velvet sap, heightened with a smartness not too overpowering; of a breast of mutton stuffed with parsley; of a loin of veal *de rivière*, thus long, white, delicate, and which is a true almond paste between the teeth; of your partridges heightened with a surprising *goût*; and then by way of farce or entertainment, of a soup with jelly broth, fortified with a young plump turkey-pout, cantoned with pigeons, and garnished with white onions married to succory. But, for my part, I confess to you my ignorance; and, as Monsieur Jourdain has very well said, I wish the repast were more worthy of your acceptance.

DORIMÈNE.   I make no other answer to this compliment than eating as I do.

M. JOURDAIN.   Ah! what pretty hands are there!

DORIMÈNE.   The hands are so so, Monsieur Jourdain; but you mean to speak of the diamond, which is very pretty.

M. JOURDAIN.   I, madame? Marry, Heaven forbid I should speak of it; I should not act like a gentleman of gallantry, and the diamond is a very trifle.

DORIMÈNE.   You are wondrous nice.

M. JOURDAIN.   You have too much goodness—

DORANTE.   [*Having made signs to* M. JOURDAIN] Come, give some wine to Monsieur Jourdain, and to those gentlemen who will do us the favour to sing us a catch.

DORIMÈNE.   You give a wondrous relish to the good cheer by mixing music with it; I am admirably well regaled here.

M. JOURDAIN.   Madame, it is not—

DORANTE.   Monsieur Jourdain, let us listen to these gentlemen, they'll entertain us with something better than all we can possibly say.

FIRST AND SECOND MUSICIANS.   [*Together, each with a glass in his hand*]

> *Put it round, my dear Phyllis, invert the bright glass;*
> *Oh what charms to the crystal those fingers impart!*
> *You and Bacchus combined, all resistance surpass,*
> *And with passion redoubled have ravished my heart.*
> *'Twixt him, you, and me, my charmer, my fair,*
> *Eternal affection let's swear.*
>
> *At the touch of those lips how he sparkles more bright!*
> *And his touch, in return, those lips does embellish:*
> *I could quaff 'em all day, and drink bumpers all night.*
> *What longing each gives me, what gusto, what relish!*
> *'Twixt him, you, and me, my charmer, my fair,*
> *Eternal affection let's swear.*

SECOND AND THIRD MUSICIANS.   [*Together*]

> *Since time flies so nimbly away,*
> *Come drink, my dear boys, drink about;*
> *Let's husband him well while we may,*
> *For life may be gone before the mug's out.*
> *When Charon has got us aboard,*
> *Our drinking and wooing are past;*
> *We ne'er to lose time can afford,*
> *For drinking's a trade not always to last.*

> *Let your puzzling rogues in the schools,*
> > *Dispute of the* bonum *of man;*
> *Philosophers dry are but fools—*
> > *The secret is this: drink, drink off your can.*
> *When Charon has got us aboard,*
> > *Our drinking and wooing are past;*
> *We ne'er to lose time can afford,*
> > *For drinking's a trade not always to last.*

ALL THREE.   [*Together*]

> *Why bob there! some wine, boys! come fill the glass, fill,*
> *Round and round let it go, till we bid it stand still.*

DORIMÈNE.   I don't think anything can be better sung; and 'tis extremely fine.

M. JOURDAIN.   I see something here though, madame, much finer.

DORIMÈNE.   Hey! Monsieur Jourdain is more gallant than I thought he was.

DORANTE.   How, madame! who do you take Monsieur Jourdain for?

M. JOURDAIN.   I wish she would take me for what I could name.

DORIMÈNE.   Again?

DORANTE.   [*To* DORIMÈNE] You don't know him.

M. JOURDAIN.   She shall know me whenever she pleases.

DORIMÈNE.   Oh! Too much.

DORANTE.   He's one who has a repartee always at hand. But you don't see, madame, that Monsieur Jourdain eats all the pieces you have touched.

DORIMÈNE.   Monsieur Jourdain is a man that I am charmed with.

M. JOURDAIN.   If I could charm your heart, I should be—

Scene II.

MME. JOURDAIN, M. JOURDAIN, DORIMÈNE, DORANTE, SINGERS, LACKEYS.

MME. JOURDAIN.   Hey-day! why here's a jolly company of you, and I see very well you did not expect me. It was for this pretty affair, then, Monsieur Husband o' mine, that you were in such a violent hurry to pack me off to dine with my sister; I just now found a play-house below, and here I find a dinner fit for a wedding. Thus it is you spend your money, and thus it is you feast the ladies in my absence, and present 'em with music and a play, whilst I'm sent abroad in the meantime.

DORANTE. What do you mean, Madame Jourdain? and what's your fancy to take it into your head that your husband spends his money, and that 'tis he who entertains my lady? Know, pray, that 'tis I do it, that he only lends me his house, and that you ought to consider a little better what you say.

M. JOURDAIN. Yes, Madame Impertinence, 'tis the count that presents the lady with all this, who is a person of quality. He does me the honour to borrow my house, and is pleased to let me be with him.

MME. JOURDAIN. 'Tis all stuff, this. I know what I know.

DORANTE. Madame Jourdain, take your best spectacles, take 'em.

MME. JOURDAIN. I've no need of spectacles, sir, I see clear enough; I've smelt things out a great while ago, I am no ass. 'Tis base in you, who are a great lord, to lend a helping hand, as you do, to the follies of my husband. And you, madame, who are a great lady, 'tis neither handsome nor honest in you to sow dissension in a family, and to suffer my husband to be in love with you.

DORIMÈNE. What can be the meaning of all this? Go, Dorante, 'tis wrong in you to expose me to the silly visions of this raving woman.

DORANTE. Madame, why madame, where are you running?

M. JOURDAIN. Madame—My lord, make my excuses to her and endeavour to bring her back.

Scene III.

MME. JOURDAIN, M. JOURDAIN, LACKEYS.

M. JOURDAIN. [*To* MME. JOURDAIN] Ah! impertinent creature as you are, these are your fine doings; you come and affront me in the face of all the world, and drive people of quality away from my house.

MME. JOURDAIN. I value not their quality.

M. JOURDAIN. [LACKEYS *take away the table*] I don't know what hinders me, you plaguy hussy, from splitting your skull with the fragments of the feast you came here to disturb.

MME. JOURDAIN. [*Going*] I despise all this. I defend my own rights, and I shall have all the wives on my side.

M. JOURDAIN. You do well to get out of the way of my fury.

Scene IV.

M. JOURDAIN (*alone*).

She came here at a most unlucky time. I was in the humour of saying fine things, and never did I find myself so witty. What have we got here?

Scene V.

M. JOURDAIN, COVIELLE (*in disguise*).

COVIELLE.   Sir, I don't know whether I have the honour to be known to you.

M. JOURDAIN.   No, sir.

COVIELLE.   I have seen you when you were not above thus tall.

M. JOURDAIN.   Me?

COVIELLE.   Yes. You were one of the prettiest children in the world; and all the ladies used to take you in their arms to kiss you.

M. JOURDAIN.   To kiss me?

COVIELLE.   Yes, I was an intimate friend of the late gentleman your father.

M. JOURDAIN.   Of the late gentleman my father!

COVIELLE.   Yes. He was a very honest gentleman.

M. JOURDAIN.   What is't you say?

COVIELLE.   I say that he was a very honest gentleman.

M. JOURDAIN.   My father?

COVIELLE.   Yes.

M. JOURDAIN.   Did you know him very well?

COVIELLE.   Certainly.

M. JOURDAIN.   And did you know him for a gentleman?

COVIELLE.   Without doubt.

M. JOURDAIN.   I don't know then what the world means.

COVIELLE.   How?

M. JOURDAIN.   There is a stupid sort of people who would face me down that he was a tradesman.

COVIELLE.   He a tradesman? 'Tis mere scandal; he never was one. All that he did was, that he was very obliging, very officious, and as he was a great connoisseur in stuffs, he used to pick them up everywhere, have 'em carried to his house, and gave 'em to his friends for money.

M. JOURDAIN.   I'm very glad of your acquaintance, that you may bear witness that my father was a gentleman.

COVIELLE.   I'll maintain it in the face of all the world.

M. JOURDAIN.   You will oblige me. What business brings you here?

COVIELLE.   Since my acquaintance with the late gentleman your father, honest gentleman, as I was telling you, I have travelled round the world.

M. JOURDAIN.   Round the world?

COVIELLE.   Yes.

M. JOURDAIN.   I fancy 'tis a huge way off, that same country.

COVIELLE.   Most certainly. I have not been returned from these tedious travels of mine but four days. And because I have an interest in everything that concerns you, I come to tell you the best news in the world.

M. JOURDAIN. What?

COVIELLE. You know that the son of the Great Turk is here.

M. JOURDAIN. I? No.

COVIELLE. How? He has a most magnificent train. All the world goes to see him, and he has been received in this country as a person of importance.

M. JOURDAIN. In troth, I did not know that.

COVIELLE. What is of advantage to you in this affair is that he is in love with your daughter.

M. JOURDAIN. The son of the Great Turk?

COVIELLE. Yes, and wants to be your son-in-law.

M. JOURDAIN. My son-in-law, the son of the Great Turk?

COVIELLE. The son of the Great Turk your son-in-law. As I have been to see him, and perfectly understand his language, he held a conversation with me; and after some other discourse, says he to me: "Acciam croc soler, onch alla moustaph gidelum amanahem varahini oussere carbulath." That is to say, "Have you not seen a young handsome person, who is the daughter of Monsieur Jourdain, a gentleman of Paris?"

M. JOURDAIN. The son of the Great Turk said that of me?

COVIELLE. Yes, as I made answer to him that I knew you particularly well, and that I had seen your daughter. Ah, says he to me, "Marababa sahem"; that is to say, "Ah! how am I enamoured with her!"

M. JOURDAIN. "Marababa sahem" means: "Ah! how am I enamoured with her"?

COVIELLE. Yes.

M. JOURDAIN. Marry, you did well to tell me so, for as for my part, I should never have believed that "Marababa sahem" had meant, "Ah! how am I enamoured with her!" 'Tis an admirable language, this same Turkish!

COVIELLE. More admirable than one can believe. Do you know very well what is the meaning of "Cacaramouchen"?

M. JOURDAIN. "Cacaramouchen"? No.

COVIELLE. 'Tis as if you should say, "My dear soul."

M. JOURDAIN. "Cacaramouchen" means, "My dear soul"?

COVIELLE. Yes.

M. JOURDAIN. Why, 'tis very wonderful! "Cacaramouchen—my dear soul." Would one ever have thought it? I am perfectly confounded at it.

COVIELLE. In short, to finish my embassy, he comes to demand your daughter in marriage; and to have a father-in-law who should be suitable to him, he designs to make you a Mamamouchi, which is a certain grand dignity of his country.

M. JOURDAIN.   Mamamouchi?

COVIELLE.   Yes, Mamamouchi; that is to say, in our language, a Paladin. Paladin is your ancient—Paladin, in short—there's nothing in the world more noble than this; and you will rank with the grandest lord upon earth.

M. JOURDAIN.   The son of the Great Turk does me a great deal of honour, and I desire you would carry me to him, to return him my thanks.

COVIELLE.   How? Why he's just acoming hither.

M. JOURDAIN.   Is he acoming hither?

COVIELLE.   Yes. And he brings all things along with him for the ceremony of your dignity.

M. JOURDAIN.   He's main hasty.

COVIELLE.   His love will suffer no delay.

M. JOURDAIN.   All that perplexes me, in this case, is that my daughter is an obstinate hussy who has took into her head one Cléonte, and vows she'll marry no person besides him.

COVIELLE.   She'll change her opinion when she sees the son of the Grand Turk; and then there happens here a very marvellous adventure, that is, that the son of the Grand Turk resembles this Cléonte, with a trifling difference. I just now came from him, they showed him me; and the love she bears for one may easily pass to the other, and—I hear him coming; there he is.

Scene VI.

CLÉONTE (*dressed as a Turk*), *three* PAGES
(*bearing* CLÉONTE's *Turkish waistcoat*), M. JOURDAIN, COVIELLE.

CLÉONTE.   Ambousahim oqui boraf, Iordina, salamalequi.

COVIELLE.   [*To* M. JOURDAIN] That is to say, Monsieur Jourdain, "May your heart be all the year like a rose-tree in flower!" These are obliging ways of speaking in that country.

M. JOURDAIN.   I am His Turkish Highness's most humble servant.

COVIELLE.   Carigar camboto oustin moraf.

CLÉONTE.   Oustin yoc catamalequi basum base alla moran.

COVIELLE.   He says, "Heaven give you the strength of lions and the prudence of serpents!"

M. JOURDAIN.   His Turkish Highness does me too much honour; and I wish him all manner of prosperity.

COVIELLE.   Ossa binamin sadoc babally oracaf ouram.

CLÉONTE.   Bel-men.

COVIELLE.   He says that you should go quickly with him to prepare yourself for the ceremony, in order afterwards to see your daughter and to conclude the marriage.

M. JOURDAIN.   So many things in two words?

COVIELLE.   Yes, the Turkish language is much in that way; it says a great deal in a few words. Go quickly where he desires you.

Scene VII.

COVIELLE (*alone*).

COVIELLE.   Ha, ha, ha. I'faith, this is all absolutely droll. What a dupe! Had he had his part by heart, he could not have played it better. O, ho!

Scene VIII.

DORANTE, COVIELLE.

COVIELLE.   I beseech you, sir, lend us a helping hand here, in a certain affair which is in agitation.

DORANTE.   Ah! ah! Covielle, who could have known thee? How art thou trimmed out there!

COVIELLE.   You see, ha, ha!

DORANTE.   What do ye laugh at?

COVIELLE.   At a thing, sir, that well deserves it.

DORANTE.   What?

COVIELLE.   I could give you a good many times, sir, to guess the stratagem we are making use of with Monsieur Jourdain, to bring him over to give his daughter to my master.

DORANTE.   I don't at all guess the stratagem, but I guess it will not fail of its effect, since you undertake it.

COVIELLE.   I know, sir, you are not unacquainted with the animal.

DORANTE.   Tell me what it is.

COVIELLE.   Be at the trouble of withdrawing a little farther off, to make room for what I see acoming. You will see one part of the story whilst I give you a narration of the rest.

Scene IX.

THE TURKISH CEREMONY

The Mufti, Dervishes, Turks (*assisting the* Mufti),
Singers, *and* Dancers.

Six Turks *enter gravely, two and two, to the sound of instruments.
They bear three carpets, with which they dance in several figures,
and then lift them up very high.* The Turks, *singing, pass under
the carpets and range themselves on each side of the stage. The*
Mufti, *accompanied by* Dervishes, *closes the march.*

Then the Turks *spread the carpets on the ground and kneel down
upon them, the* Mufti *and the* Dervishes *standing in the
middle of them; while the* Mufti *invokes Mahomet in dumb con-
tortions and grimaces,* the Turks *prostrate themselves to the
ground, singing Allah, raising their hands in heaven, singing
Allah, and so continuing alternately to the end of the invocation,
when they all rise up, singing Allahekber.*

Scene X.

Mufti, Dervishes, Turks (*who sing and dance*), M. Jourdain
(*dressed in Turkish style, his head shaved, without turban or saber*).

Mufti.   [*To* M. Jourdain]

> If thou understandest,
>   Answer;
> If thou dost not understand,
>   Hold thy peace, hold thy peace.

> I am Mufti,
>   Thou! who thou art
> I don't know:
>   Hold thy peace, hold thy peace.

Scene XI.

Mufti, Dervishes, Turks (*who sing and dance*).

Mufti.   Say, Turk, who is this,
            An Anabaptist, an Anabaptist?
The Turks.   No.

MUFTI.   A Zwinglian?
THE TURKS.   No.
MUFTI.   A Coffite?
THE TURKS.   No.
MUFTI.   A Hussite? A Morist? A Fronist?
THE TURKS.   No, no, no.
MUFTI.   No, no, no. Is he a Pagan?
THE TURKS.   No.
MUFTI.   A Lutheran?
THE TURKS.   No.
MUFTI.   A Puritan?
THE TURKS.   No.
MUFTI.   A Brahmin? A Moffian? A Zurian?
THE TURKS.   No, no, no.
MUFTI.   No, no, no. A Mahometan, a Mahometan?
THE TURKS.   There you have it, there you have it.
MUFTI.   How is he called? How is he called?
THE TURKS.   Jourdain, Jourdain.
MUFTI.   [*Dancing*] Jourdain! Jourdain!
THE TURKS.   Jourdain, Jourdain.
MUFTI.

> *To Mahomet for Jourdain*
> *I pray night and day,*
> *That he would make a Paladin*
> *Of Jourdain, of Jourdain.*
> *Give him a turban, and give a sabre,*
> *With a galley and a brigantine,*
> *To defend Palestine.*
> *To Mahomet for Jourdain*
> *I pray night and day.*

[*To* THE TURKS] Is Jourdain a good Turk?
THE TURKS.   That he is, that he is.
MUFTI.   [*Singing and dancing*]

> *Ha, la ba, ba la chou, ba la ba, ba la da.*

THE TURKS.

> *Ha, la ba, ba la chou, ba la ba, ba la da.*

Scene XII.

TURKS (*who sing and dance*).

Scene XIII.

MUFTI, DERVISHES, M. JOURDAIN, TURKS (*who sing and dance*).

The MUFTI *returns with the State Turban, which is of an immeasurable largeness, garnished with lighted wax candles, four or five rows deep, accompanied by two* DERVISHES, *bearing the Alcoran, with comic caps garnished also with lighted candles.*

The two other DERVISHES *lead up* M. JOURDAIN *and place him on his knees with his hands to the ground so that his back, on which the Alcoran is placed, may serve for a desk to the* MUFTI, *who makes a second burlesque invocation, knitting his eyebrows, striking his hands sometimes upon the Alcoran, and tossing over the leaves with precipitation, after which, lifting up his hands, and crying with a loud voice,* Hoo.

During *this second invocation the assistant* TURKS, *bowing down and raising themselves alternately, sing likewise,*

HOO, HOO, HOO.

M. JOURDAIN.   [*After they have taken the Alcoran off his back*] Ouf!

MUFTI.   [*To* M. JOURDAIN] Thou wilt not be a knave?

THE TURKS.   No, no, no.

MUFTI.   Not be a thief?

THE TURKS.   No, no, no.

MUFTI.   [*To* THE TURKS] Give the turban.

THE TURKS.   [*Putting the turban on* M. JOURDAIN's *head*]

> Thou wilt not be a knave?
>   No, no, no.
> Not be a thief?
>   No, no, no.
> Give the turban.

MUFTI.   [*Giving the sabre to* M. JOURDAIN]

> Be brave, be no scoundrel,
> Take the sabre.

THE TURKS.   [*Drawing their sabres*]

> Be brave, be no scoundrel,
> Take the sabre.

[THE TURKS, *dancing, strike* M. JOURDAIN *several times with their sabres, to music*]

MUFTI.

> *Give, give*
> *The bastonade.*

THE TURKS.

> *Give, give*
> *The bastonade.*

[THE TURKS, *dancing, give* M. JOURDAIN *several strokes with a cudgel, to music*]

MUFTI.

> *Don't think it a shame,*
> *This is the last affront.*

THE TURKS.

> *Don't think it a shame,*
> *This is the last affront.*

[*The* MUFTI *begins a third invocation. The* DERVISHES *support him with great respect, after which* THE TURKS, *singing and dancing round the* MUFTI, *retire with him and lead off* M. JOURDAIN.]

Act V.

Scene I.

MME. JOURDAIN, M. JOURDAIN.

MME. JOURDAIN.   Bless us all! Mercy upon us! What have we got here? What a figure! What! dressed to go a-mumming, and is this a time to go masked? Speak therefore, what does this mean? Who has trussed you up in this manner?

M. JOURDAIN.   Do but see the impertinent slut, to speak after this manner to a Mamamouchi.

MME. JOURDAIN.   How's that?

M. JOURDAIN.   Yes, you must show me respect now I am just made a Mamamouchi.

MME. JOURDAIN.   What d'ye mean with your Mamamouchi?

M. JOURDAIN.   Mamamouchi, I tell you. I am a Mamamouchi.

MME. JOURDAIN.   What beast is that?

M. JOURDAIN.   Mamamouchi, that is to say, in our language, a Paladin.

MME. JOURDAIN.   A Paladin? Are you of an age to be a morris-dancer?

M. JOURDAIN.   What an ignoramus! I say, Paladin. 'Tis a dignity of which I have just now gone through the ceremony.

MME. JOURDAIN.   What ceremony then?

M. JOURDAIN.   Mahameta per Jordina.

MME. JOURDAIN.   What does that mean?

M. JOURDAIN.   Jordina, that is to say, Jourdain.

MME. JOURDAIN.   Well, how Jourdain?

M. JOURDAIN.   Voler far un Paladina de Jordina.

MME. JOURDAIN.   What?

M. JOURDAIN.   Dar turbanta con galera.

MME. JOURDAIN.   What's the meaning of that?

M. JOURDAIN.   Per deffender Palestina.

MME. JOURDAIN.   What is it you would say?

M. JOURDAIN.   Dara, dara, bastonnara.

MME. JOURDAIN.   What is this same jargon?

M. JOURDAIN.   Non tener honta, questa star l'ultima affronta.

MME. JOURDAIN.   What in the name of wonder can all this be?

M. JOURDAIN.   [*Singing and dancing*] Hou la ba, ba la chou, ba la ba, ba la da. [*Falls down to the ground*]

MME. JOURDAIN.   Alas and well-a-day! My husband is turned fool.

M. JOURDAIN.   [*Getting up and walking off*] Peace! insolence, show respect to Monsieur Mamamouchi.

MME. JOURDAIN.   [*Alone*] How could he lose his senses? I must run and prevent his going out. [*Seeing* DORIMÈNE *and* DORANTE] So, so, here come the rest of our gang. I see nothing but vexation on all sides.

Scene II.

DORANTE, DORIMÈNE.

DORANTE.   Yes, madame, you'll see the merriest thing that can be seen; and I don't believe it's possible, in the whole world, to find another man so much a fool as this here. And besides, madame, we must endeavour to promote Cléonte's amour and to countenance his masquerade. He's a very pretty gentleman and deserves that one should interest one's self in his favour.

DORIMÈNE.   I've a very great value for him, and he deserves good fortune.

DORANTE.   Besides, we have here, madame, an entertainment that will suit us, and which we ought not to suffer to be lost; and I must by all means see whether my fancy will succeed.

DORIMÈNE.   I saw there magnificent preparations, and these are things, Dorante, I can no longer suffer. Yes, I'm resolved to put a stop, at last, to your profusions; and to break off all the expenses you are at on my account, I have determined to marry you out of hand. This is the real secret of the affair, and all these things end, as you know, with marriage.

DORANTE.   Ah! madame, is it possible you should form so kind a resolution in my favour?

DORIMÈNE.   I only do it to prevent you from ruining yourself; and without this, I see plainly that before 'tis long you won't be worth a groat.

DORANTE.   How am I obliged to you, madame, for the care you take to preserve my estate! 'Tis entirely at your service, as well as my heart, and you may use both of 'em just in the manner you please.

DORIMÈNE.   I shall make a proper use of them both. But here comes your man; an admirable figure.

Scene III.

M. JOURDAIN, DORANTE, DORIMÈNE.

DORANTE.   Sir, my lady and I are come to pay our homage to your new dignity, and to rejoice with you at the marriage you are concluding betwixt your daughter and the son of the Grand Turk.

M. JOURDAIN.   [*Bowing first in the Turkish manner*] Sir, I wish you the force of serpents and the wisdom of lions.

DORIMÈNE.   I was exceeding glad to be one of the first, sir, who should come and congratulate you upon the high degree of glory to which you are raised.

M. JOURDAIN.   Madame, I wish your rose-tree may flower all the year round; I am infinitely obliged to you for interesting yourselves in the honour that's paid me; and I am greatly rejoiced to see you returned hither, that I may make my most humble excuses for the impertinence of my wife.

DORIMÈNE.   That's nothing at all, I can excuse a commotion of this kind in her; your heart ought to be precious to her, and 'tis not at all strange the possession of such a man as you are should give her some alarms.

M. JOURDAIN.   The possession of my heart is a thing you have entirely gained.

DORANTE.   You see, madame, that Monsieur Jourdain is none of those people whom prosperity blinds, and that he knows, in all his grandeur, how to own his friends.

DORIMÈNE.   'Tis the mark of a truly generous soul.

DORANTE.   Where is His Turkish Highness? We should be glad, as your friends, to pay our devoirs to him.

M. JOURDAIN.   There he comes, and I have sent to bring my daughter to join hands with him.

Scene IV.

M. JOURDAIN, DORIMÈNE, DORANTE, CLÉONTE (*dressed as a Turk*).

DORANTE.   [*To* CLÉONTE] Sir, we come to compliment Your Highness, as friends of the gentleman your father-in-law, and to assure you, with respect, of our most humble services.

M. JOURDAIN.   Where's the dragoman, to tell him who you are and make him understand what you say? You shall see that he'll answer you, and he speaks Turkish marvellously. Hola! there; where the deuce is he gone? [*To* CLÉONTE] Stref, strif, strof, straf.

The gentleman is a
>   *grande segnore, grande segnore, grande segnore;*
and madame is a
>   *granda dama, granda dama.*

[*Seeing he cannot make himself be understood*] Lack-a-day! [*To* CLÉONTE] Sir, he be a French Mamamouchi, and madame a French Mamamouchess. I can't speak plainer. Good, here's the dragoman.

Scene V.

M. JOURDAIN, DORIMÈNE, CLÉONTE (*dressed as a Turk*),
COVIELLE (*in disguise*).

M. JOURDAIN.   Where do you run? We can say nothing without you. [*Pointing to* CLÉONTE] Inform him a little that the gentleman and lady are persons of great quality who come to pay their compliments to him, as friends of mine, and to assure him of their services. [*To* DORIMÈNE *and* DORANTE] You shall see how he will answer.

COVIELLE.   Alabala crociam, acci boram alabamen.

CLÉONTE.   Catalequi tubal ourin soter amalouchan.

M. JOURDAIN.   [*To* DORIMÈNE *and* DORANTE] Do ye see?

COVIELLE.   He says that the rain of prosperity waters, at all seasons, the garden of your family.

M. JOURDAIN.   I told you that he speaks Turkish.

DORANTE.   This is admirable.

Scene VI.

LUCILE, CLÉONTE, M. JOURDAIN, DORIMÈNE, DORANTE, COVIELLE.

M. JOURDAIN.   Come, daughter, come nearer, and give the gentleman your hand who does you the honour of demanding you in marriage.

LUCILE.   What's the matter, father, how are you dressed here? What! are you playing a comedy?

M. JOURDAIN.   No, no, 'tis no comedy, 'tis a very serious affair; and the most honourable for you that possibly can be wished. [*Pointing to* CLÉONTE] This is the husband I bestow upon you.

LUCILE.   Upon me, father?

M. JOURDAIN.   Yes, upon you. Come, take him by the hand, and thank Heaven for your good fortune.

LUCILE.   I won't marry.

M. JOURDAIN.   I'll make you; am I not your father?

LUCILE.   I won't do it.

M. JOURDAIN.   Here's a noise indeed! Come, I tell you. Your hand here.

LUCILE.   No, father, I've told you before that there's no power can oblige me to take any other husband than Cléonte; and I am determined upon all extremities rather than—[*Discovering* CLÉONTE] 'Tis true that you are my father; I owe you absolute obedience; and you may dispose of me according to your pleasure.

M. JOURDAIN.   Hah, I am charmed to see you return so readily to your duty; and it is a pleasure to me to have my daughter obedient.

Scene VII.

MME. JOURDAIN, CLÉONTE, M. JOURDAIN,
LUCILE, DORANTE, DORIMÈNE, COVIELLE.

MME. JOURDAIN.   How, how, what does this mean? They tell me you design to marry your daughter to a mummer.

M. JOURDAIN.   Will you hold your tongue, impertinence? You're always coming to mix your extravagances with everything; there's no possibility of teaching you common sense.

MME. JOURDAIN.   'Tis you whom there's no teaching to be wise, and you go from folly to folly. What's your design, what would you do with this flock of people?

M. JOURDAIN.   I design to marry my daughter to the son of the Grand Turk.

MME. JOURDAIN.   To the son of the Grand Turk?

M. JOURDAIN.   [*Pointing to* COVIELLE] Make your compliments to him by the dragoman there.

MME. JOURDAIN.   I have nothing to do with the dragoman, and I shall tell him plainly to his face that he shall have none of my daughter.

M. JOURDAIN.   Will you hold your tongue once more?

DORANTE.   What, Madame Jourdain, do you oppose such an honour as this? Do you refuse His Turkish Highness for a son-in-law?

MME. JOURDAIN.   Lack-a-day, sir, meddle you with your own affairs.

DORIMÈNE.   'Tis a great honour, 'tis by no means to be rejected.

MME. JOURDAIN.   Madame, I desire you too not to give yourself any trouble about what no ways concerns you.

DORANTE. 'Tis the friendship we have for you that makes us interest ourselves in what is of advantage to you.

MME. JOURDAIN. I shall easily excuse your friendship.

DORANTE. There's your daughter consents to her father's pleasure.

MME. JOURDAIN. My daughter consent to marry a Turk?

DORANTE. Certainly.

MME. JOURDAIN. Can she forget Cléonte?

DORANTE. What would one not do to be a great lady?

MME. JOURDAIN. I would strangle her with my own hands, had she done such a thing as this.

M. JOURDAIN. Here's tittle-tattle in abundance. I tell you this marriage shall be consummated.

MME. JOURDAIN. And I tell you that it shall not be consummated.

M. JOURDAIN. What a noise is here?

LUCILE. Mother!

MME. JOURDAIN. Go, you are a pitiful hussy.

M. JOURDAIN. [*To* MME. JOURDAIN] What! do you scold her for being obedient to me?

MME. JOURDAIN. Yes, she belongs to me as well as you.

COVIELLE. [*To* MME. JOURDAIN] Madame.

MME. JOURDAIN. What would you say to me, you?

COVIELLE. One word.

MME. JOURDAIN. I've nothing to do with your word.

COVIELLE. [*To* M. JOURDAIN] Sir, would she hear me but one word in private, I'll promise you to make her consent to what you have a mind.

MME. JOURDAIN. I won't consent to it.

COVIELLE. Only hear me.

MME. JOURDAIN. No.

M. JOURDAIN. [*To* MME. JOURDAIN] Give him the hearing.

MME. JOURDAIN. No, I won't hear him.

M. JOURDAIN. He'll tell you—

MME. JOURDAIN. He shall tell me nothing.

M. JOURDAIN. Do but see the great obstinacy of the woman! Will it do you any harm to hear him?

COVIELLE. Only hear me; you may do what you please afterwards.

MME. JOURDAIN. Well, what?

COVIELLE. [*Aside to* MME. JOURDAIN] We have made signs to you, madame, this hour. Don't you see plainly that all is done purely to accommodate ourselves to the visions of your husband; that we are imposing upon him under this disguise, and that it is Cléonte himself who is the son of the Great Turk?

MME. JOURDAIN. [*Aside to* COVIELLE] Oh, oh?

COVIELLE.   [*Aside to* MME. JOURDAIN] And that 'tis me, Covielle, who am the dragoman?

MME. JOURDAIN.   [*Aside to* COVIELLE] Oh! in that case, I give up.

COVIELLE.   [*Aside to* MME. JOURDAIN] Don't seem to know anything of the matter.

MME. JOURDAIN.   [*Aloud*] Yes, 'tis all done, I consent to the marriage.

M. JOURDAIN.   Ay, all the world submits to reason. [*To* MME. JOURDAIN] You would not hear him. I knew he would explain to you what the son of the Great Turk is.

MME. JOURDAIN.   He has explained it to me sufficiently, and I'm satisfied with it. Let us send for a notary.

DORANTE.   'Tis well said. And, Madame Jourdain, that you may set your mind perfectly at rest, and that you should this day quit all jealousy which you may have entertained of the gentleman your husband, my lady and I shall make use of the same notary to marry us.

MME. JOURDAIN.   I consent to that too.

M. JOURDAIN.   [*Aside to* DORANTE] 'Tis to make her believe.

DORANTE.   [*Aside to* M. JOURDAIN] We must by all means amuse her a little with this pretence.

M. JOURDAIN.   Good, good. [*Aloud*] Let somebody go for the notary.

DORANTE.   In the meantime, till he comes and has drawn up the contracts, let us see our entertainment, and give His Turkish Highness the diversion of it.

M. JOURDAIN.   Well advised; come let us take our places.

MME. JOURDAIN.   And Nicole?

M. JOURDAIN.   I give her to the dragoman; and my wife, to whosoever pleases to take her.

COVIELLE.   Sir, I thank you. [*Aside*] If it's possible to find a greater fool than this, I'll go and publish it in Rome.

DOVER · THRIFT · EDITIONS

POETRY

A SHROPSHIRE LAD, A. E. Housman. 64pp. 26468-8 $1.00

LYRIC POEMS, John Keats. 80pp. 26871-3 $1.00

GUNGA DIN AND OTHER FAVORITE POEMS, Rudyard Kipling. 80pp. 26471-8 $1.00

THE CONGO AND OTHER POEMS, Vachel Lindsay. 96pp. 27272-9 $1.50

EVANGELINE AND OTHER POEMS, Henry Wadsworth Longfellow. 64pp. 28255-4 $1.00

FAVORITE POEMS, Henry Wadsworth Longfellow. 96pp. 27273-7 $1.00

"TO HIS COY MISTRESS" AND OTHER POEMS, Andrew Marvell. 64pp. 29544-3 $1.00

SPOON RIVER ANTHOLOGY, Edgar Lee Masters. 144pp. 27275-3 $1.50

RENASCENCE AND OTHER POEMS, Edna St. Vincent Millay. 64pp. (Available in U.S. only.) 26873-X $1.00

SELECTED POEMS, John Milton. 128pp. 27554-X $1.50

CIVIL WAR POETRY: An Anthology, Paul Negri (ed.). 128pp. 29883-3 $1.50

ENGLISH VICTORIAN POETRY: AN ANTHOLOGY, Paul Negri (ed.). 256pp. 40425-0 $2.00

GREAT SONNETS, Paul Negri (ed.). 96pp. 28052-7 $1.00

THE RAVEN AND OTHER FAVORITE POEMS, Edgar Allan Poe. 64pp. 26685-0 $1.00

ESSAY ON MAN AND OTHER POEMS, Alexander Pope. 128pp. 28053-5 $1.50

EARLY POEMS, Ezra Pound. 80pp. (Available in U.S. only.) 28745-9 $1.00

GREAT POEMS BY AMERICAN WOMEN: An Anthology, Susan L. Rattiner (ed.). 224pp. (Available in U.S. only.) 40164-2 $2.00

LITTLE ORPHANT ANNIE AND OTHER POEMS, James Whitcomb Riley. 80pp. 28260-0 $1.00

"MINIVER CHEEVY" AND OTHER POEMS, Edwin Arlington Robinson. 64pp. 28756-4 $1.00

GOBLIN MARKET AND OTHER POEMS, Christina Rossetti. 64pp. 28055-1 $1.00

CHICAGO POEMS, Carl Sandburg. 80pp. 28057-8 $1.00

THE SHOOTING OF DAN MCGREW AND OTHER POEMS, Robert Service. 96pp. (Available in U.S. only.) 27556-6 $1.50

COMPLETE SONNETS, William Shakespeare. 80pp. 26686-9 $1.00

SELECTED POEMS, Percy Bysshe Shelley. 128pp. 27558-2 $1.50

AFRICAN-AMERICAN POETRY: An Anthology, 1773–1930, Joan R. Sherman (ed.). 96pp. 29604-0 $1.00

100 BEST-LOVED POEMS, Philip Smith (ed.). 96pp. 28553-7 $1.00

NATIVE AMERICAN SONGS AND POEMS: An Anthology, Brian Swann (ed.). 64pp. 29450-1 $1.00

SELECTED POEMS, Alfred Lord Tennyson. 112pp. 27282-6 $1.50

AENEID, Vergil (Publius Vergilius Maro). 256pp. 28749-1 $2.00

CHRISTMAS CAROLS: COMPLETE VERSES, Shane Weller (ed.). 64pp. 27397-0 $1.00

GREAT LOVE POEMS, Shane Weller (ed.). 128pp. 27284-2 $1.00

CIVIL WAR POETRY AND PROSE, Walt Whitman. 96pp. 28507-3 $1.00

SELECTED POEMS, Walt Whitman. 128pp. 26878-0 $1.00

THE BALLAD OF READING GAOL AND OTHER POEMS, Oscar Wilde. 64pp. 27072-6 $1.00

EARLY POEMS, William Carlos Williams. 64pp. (Available in U.S. only.) 29294-0 $1.00

FAVORITE POEMS, William Wordsworth. 80pp. 27073-4 $1.00

WORLD WAR ONE BRITISH POETS: Brooke, Owen, Sassoon, Rosenberg, and Others, Candace Ward (ed.). (Available in U.S. only.) 29568-0 $1.00

EARLY POEMS, William Butler Yeats. 128pp. 27808-5 $1.50

"EASTER, 1916" AND OTHER POEMS, William Butler Yeats. 80pp. (Available in U.S. only.) 29771-3 $1.00

DOVER·THRIFT·EDITIONS

FICTION

FLATLAND: A ROMANCE OF MANY DIMENSIONS, Edwin A. Abbott. 96pp. 27263-X $1.00

SHORT STORIES, Louisa May Alcott. 64pp. 29063-8 $1.00

WINESBURG, OHIO, Sherwood Anderson. 160pp. 28269-4 $2.00

PERSUASION, Jane Austen. 224pp. 29555-9 $2.00

PRIDE AND PREJUDICE, Jane Austen. 272pp. 28473-5 $2.00

SENSE AND SENSIBILITY, Jane Austen. 272pp. 29049-2 $2.00

LOOKING BACKWARD, Edward Bellamy. 160pp. 29038-7 $2.00

BEOWULF, Beowulf (trans. by R. K. Gordon). 64pp. 27264-8 $1.00

CIVIL WAR STORIES, Ambrose Bierce. 128pp. 28038-1 $1.00

"THE MOONLIT ROAD" AND OTHER GHOST AND HORROR STORIES, Ambrose Bierce (John Grafton, ed.) 96pp. 40056-5 $1.00

WUTHERING HEIGHTS, Emily Brontë. 256pp. 29256-8 $2.00

THE THIRTY-NINE STEPS, John Buchan. 96pp. 28201-5 $1.50

TARZAN OF THE APES, Edgar Rice Burroughs. 224pp. (Available in U.S. only.) 29570-2 $2.00

ALICE'S ADVENTURES IN WONDERLAND, Lewis Carroll. 96pp. 27543-4 $1.00

THROUGH THE LOOKING-GLASS, Lewis Carroll. 128pp. 40878-7 $1.50

MY ÁNTONIA, Willa Cather. 176pp. 28240-6 $2.00

O PIONEERS!, Willa Cather. 128pp. 27785-2 $1.00

PAUL'S CASE AND OTHER STORIES, Willa Cather. 64pp. 29057-3 $1.00

FIVE GREAT SHORT STORIES, Anton Chekhov. 96pp. 26463-7 $1.00

TALES OF CONJURE AND THE COLOR LINE, Charles Waddell Chesnutt. 128pp. 40426-9 $1.50

FAVORITE FATHER BROWN STORIES, G. K. Chesterton. 96pp. 27545-0 $1.00

THE AWAKENING, Kate Chopin. 128pp. 27786-0 $1.00

A PAIR OF SILK STOCKINGS AND OTHER STORIES, Kate Chopin. 64pp. 29264-9 $1.00

HEART OF DARKNESS, Joseph Conrad. 80pp. 26464-5 $1.00

LORD JIM, Joseph Conrad. 256pp. 40650-4 $2.00

THE SECRET SHARER AND OTHER STORIES, Joseph Conrad. 128pp. 27546-9 $1.00

THE "LITTLE REGIMENT" AND OTHER CIVIL WAR STORIES, Stephen Crane. 80pp. 29557-5 $1.00

THE OPEN BOAT AND OTHER STORIES, Stephen Crane. 128pp. 27547-7 $1.50

THE RED BADGE OF COURAGE, Stephen Crane. 112pp. 26465-3 $1.00

MOLL FLANDERS, Daniel Defoe. 256pp. 29093-X $2.00

ROBINSON CRUSOE, Daniel Defoe. 288pp. 40427-7 $2.00

A CHRISTMAS CAROL, Charles Dickens. 80pp. 26865-9 $1.00

THE CRICKET ON THE HEARTH AND OTHER CHRISTMAS STORIES, Charles Dickens. 128pp. 28039-X $1.00

A TALE OF TWO CITIES, Charles Dickens. 304pp. 40651-2 $2.00

THE DOUBLE, Fyodor Dostoyevsky. 128pp. 29572-9 $1.50

THE GAMBLER, Fyodor Dostoyevsky. 112pp. 29081-6 $1.50

NOTES FROM THE UNDERGROUND, Fyodor Dostoyevsky. 96pp. 27053-X $1.00

THE ADVENTURE OF THE DANCING MEN AND OTHER STORIES, Sir Arthur Conan Doyle. 80pp. 29558-3 $1.00

THE HOUND OF THE BASKERVILLES, Arthur Conan Doyle. 128pp. 28214-7 $1.50

THE LOST WORLD, Arthur Conan Doyle. 176pp. 40060-3 $1.50

DOVER · THRIFT · EDITIONS

FICTION

SIX GREAT SHERLOCK HOLMES STORIES, Sir Arthur Conan Doyle. 112pp. 27055-6 $1.00

SILAS MARNER, George Eliot. 160pp. 29246-0 $1.50

THIS SIDE OF PARADISE, F. Scott Fitzgerald. 208pp. 28999-0 $2.00

"THE DIAMOND AS BIG AS THE RITZ" AND OTHER STORIES, F. Scott Fitzgerald. 29991-0 $2.00

THE REVOLT OF "MOTHER" AND OTHER STORIES, Mary E. Wilkins Freeman. 128pp. 40428-5 $1.50

MADAME BOVARY, Gustave Flaubert. 256pp. 29257-6 $2.00

WHERE ANGELS FEAR TO TREAD, E. M. Forster. 128pp. (Available in U.S. only.) 27791-7 $1.50

A ROOM WITH A VIEW, E. M. Forster. 176pp. (Available in U.S. only.) 28467-0 $2.00

THE IMMORALIST, André Gide. 112pp. (Available in U.S. only.) 29237-1 $1.50

"THE YELLOW WALLPAPER" AND OTHER STORIES, Charlotte Perkins Gilman. 80pp. 29857-4 $1.00

HERLAND, Charlotte Perkins Gilman. 128pp. 40429-3 $1.50

THE OVERCOAT AND OTHER STORIES, Nikolai Gogol. 112pp. 27057-2 $1.50

GREAT GHOST STORIES, John Grafton (ed.). 112pp. 27270-2 $1.00

DETECTION BY GASLIGHT, Douglas G. Greene (ed.). 272pp. 29928-7 $2.00

THE MABINOGION, Lady Charlotte E. Guest. 192pp. 29541-9 $2.00

"THE FIDDLER OF THE REELS" AND OTHER SHORT STORIES, Thomas Hardy. 80pp. 29960-0 $1.50

THE LUCK OF ROARING CAMP AND OTHER STORIES, Bret Harte. 96pp. 27271-0 $1.00

THE SCARLET LETTER, Nathaniel Hawthorne. 192pp. 28048-9 $2.00

YOUNG GOODMAN BROWN AND OTHER STORIES, Nathaniel Hawthorne. 128pp. 27060-2 $1.00

THE GIFT OF THE MAGI AND OTHER SHORT STORIES, O. Henry. 96pp. 27061-0 $1.00

THE NUTCRACKER AND THE GOLDEN POT, E. T. A. Hoffmann. 128pp. 27806-9 $1.00

THE BEAST IN THE JUNGLE AND OTHER STORIES, Henry James. 128pp. 27552-3 $1.50

DAISY MILLER, Henry James. 64pp. 28773-4 $1.00

THE TURN OF THE SCREW, Henry James. 96pp. 26684-2 $1.00

WASHINGTON SQUARE, Henry James. 176pp. 40431-5 $2.00

THE COUNTRY OF THE POINTED FIRS, Sarah Orne Jewett. 96pp. 28196-5 $1.00

THE AUTOBIOGRAPHY OF AN EX-COLORED MAN, James Weldon Johnson. 112pp. 28512-X $1.00

DUBLINERS, James Joyce. 160pp. 26870-5 $1.00

A PORTRAIT OF THE ARTIST AS A YOUNG MAN, James Joyce. 192pp. 28050-0 $2.00

THE METAMORPHOSIS AND OTHER STORIES, Franz Kafka. 96pp. 29030-1 $1.50

THE MAN WHO WOULD BE KING AND OTHER STORIES, Rudyard Kipling. 128pp. 28051-9 $1.50

YOU KNOW ME AL, Ring Lardner. 128pp. 28513-8 $1.50

SELECTED SHORT STORIES, D. H. Lawrence. 128pp. 27794-1 $1.50

GREEN TEA AND OTHER GHOST STORIES, J. Sheridan LeFanu. 96pp. 27795-X $1.50

SHORT STORIES, Theodore Dreiser. 112pp. 28215-5 $1.50

THE CALL OF THE WILD, Jack London. 64pp. 26472-6 $1.00

FIVE GREAT SHORT STORIES, Jack London. 96pp. 27063-7 $1.00

WHITE FANG, Jack London. 160pp. 26968-X $1.00

DEATH IN VENICE, Thomas Mann. 96pp. (Available in U.S. only.) 28714-9 $1.00

IN A GERMAN PENSION: 13 Stories, Katherine Mansfield. 112pp. 28719-X $1.50

THE MOON AND SIXPENCE, W. Somerset Maugham. 176pp. (Available in U.S. only.) 28731-9 $2.00